Strength to strength

Strength

to strength

Binding the threads of an unbreakable life

Marc Thompson and Barry Purcell

Prentice Hall Life
is an imprint of

Harlow, England • London • New York • Boston • San Francisco • Toronto • Sydney • Singapore • Hong Kong
Tokyo • Seoul • Taipei • New Delhi • Cape Town • Madrid • Mexico City • Amsterdam • Munich • Paris • Milan

PEARSON EDUCATION LIMITED

Edinburgh Gate
Harlow CM20 2JE
Tel: +44 (0)1279 623623
Fax: +44 (0)1279 431059
Website: www.pearsoned.co.uk

First published in Great Britain in 2010

Pearson Education is not responsible for the content of third party internet sites.

ISBN: 978-0-273-73130-6

British Library Cataloguing-in-Publication Data
A catalogue record for this book is available from the British Library

Library of Congress Cataloging-in-Publication Data
A catalog record for this book is available from the Library of Congress

10 9 8 7 6 5 4 3 2 1
14 13 12 11 10

Typeset in 10/15pt Myriad Pro by Fakenham Photosetting Limited, Fakenham, Norfolk
Printed by Ashford Colour Press Ltd, Gosport

Contents

Thank you Karyn, for being a
gleaming, Golden Thread.
Your contribution and involvement
helped make this book possible.

About the authors

MARC THOMPSON was born in Bradford and left school aged 15. After turning his back on a violent, disreputable lifestyle, he went on to found a successful telecoms company, which he sold in 2005 for a multimillion pound sum.

Marc has since founded a new telecoms company, and lives near Leeds with his wife, Jo, and two sons.

BARRY PURCELL lives in Wakefield, West Yorkshire, with his wife Janet. They have three children. After leaving his factory job, Barry went on to found a chain of health clubs across Yorkshire. Today he is a director of the food business that was co-founded by his family in 2001, with award-winning products stocked in supermarkets across the UK.

Introduction

I f life is a series of highs and lows then everyone, at some time, hits bottom.

For Barry Purcell it happened as he sat in a waiting room in a Bradford hospital, waiting to be seen by the in-house psychiatrist. The benches were hard, the linoleum was well-scrubbed and the cold air was thick with the stench of disinfectant. It was 1964 and he was 20 years old. He was young and strong; to look at him, you wouldn't have known that anything was wrong. But Barry had been led, gently, away from the factory floor on which he worked after crippling panic attacks had escalated into a nervous breakdown. When he tried to speak, he couldn't get the words out. When others spoke to him, he burst into tears. His hands shook. After he left the factory, he spent most of his time sleeping.

The only other people in that waiting room were a mother and her infant son. The child was in a state of distress. He groaned, screamed and wailed, and his desperate mother couldn't quiet him. The sounds were terrible. Barry shrank further and further into his seat.

The psychiatrist didn't know what was wrong with Barry, but questioned him at length and recommended a return visit. Sitting on the bus back to his parents' house, shoulders hunched, Barry believed that he had nowhere left to turn. He was finished.

For Marc Thompson, rock bottom came on his 32nd birthday. When he looked at the sawn-off shotgun he kept for his own protection and felt the roll of banknotes he kept in his pocket, it sank in that he was on a dangerous road going nowhere, fast. On the face of it, Marc was a success. He ran a number of thriving local businesses including pubs, clubs and a lucrative security business. He was the proud owner of a large house and a sports car, and the father of a young son. But Marc rarely stayed at that house. It wasn't even decorated. He was often wasted when his son visited, and his employees regularly had to babysit the little boy.

This wasn't the life that Marc wanted for himself. He handed the security business to his right-hand man. He gave the licence for the pub to his best friend. The guns and the drugs went. The cash went. His car was repossessed. His house was sold at a price well below its market value. He ended up back in his old bedroom at his parents' house, sleeping in a single bed. When he needed to go somewhere, he borrowed his mum's car. His decision to change his life left him deeply in debt. Where could he go from here?

***

Today, these two men are fundamentally changed.

Barry Purcell has had his ups and downs, but he has come a long way from that cold hospital waiting room. A family-run firm, which he founded with his wife and two friends in 2001, has a seven-figure turnover and produces products that are snapped up by all the major UK supermarkets. Barry has been happily married for 26 years and has three adult children. His daughter is getting married this year. He is talkative, confident and content. His hands no longer shake.

Marc Thompson is a happily married father of two. He founded a telecommunications company; in 2005 he sold it for a seven-figure sum. His spacious family home is mortgage-free. His cars are paid for. Neither Marc nor his wife needs to work; instead they spend a lot of time with their sons and their friends.

These changes haven't happened overnight. Barry and Marc have worked hard to understand how to build successful lives and how to make each part of their lives resilient, so that they now have success built on strong foundations.

This book shares the lives of the authors and the knowledge they have gained on their journeys and gives you the steps to build a similarly successful life. It doesn't matter where you are starting from. You could be the CEO of a FTSE 100 company; you could be unemployed. And it doesn't matter how old you are, what your qualifications are or what your experience of the working world has been. The only qualification you need is a willingness to change and progress.

***

Our lives are made up of threads intertwining throughout our existence. A thread can be many things: a person, a book, an achievement, a spark of inspiration, satisfying work, a loving relationship, a productive habit, or even a tip-off from a friend.

When they are nurtured they become golden strands, supporting you throughout your life. Weave them together and they form an unbreakable rope, which will enable you to climb from where you are to where you want to be.

In this book we have divided these threads into the eight key areas of life: Learning, Career, Wealth, Productivity, Health, Relationships, Family, Spiritual. In each section we give you the best insights, inspirational stories, action points and worksheets so by the end of the section you will have a better understanding of that area of your life and how to progress towards making each thread golden.

Marc Thompson and Barry Purcell both fell hard. But they worked their Golden Threads into Golden Ropes, and climbed those ropes towards the sky. The old Barry and the old Marc fell away beneath them; their debts diminished and disappeared; their troubles shrank as their successes and achievements multiplied. They're still climbing.

If you'd like to do the same, read on.

CHAPTER 1

The rope maker

Your potential is infinite when you are always learning, always trying, always believing in yourself and your Golden Threads. Your goals may be ambitious and your ambitions may be formidable. That thirst, created by passion and drive, will take you wherever you want to go.

This first chapter of this book is called 'The rope maker', because the only person who can build your Golden Rope is you. Drawing upon your imagination, you have the power to think and create your future.

Don't wait for others to make your plans, and don't wait for opportunities to come knocking on your door: what if they don't show up? Paratroopers always insist on packing their own parachutes; likewise, you should resist the temptation to place your fate in another person's hands. You are the rope maker: it is down to you to take hold of the strands running through your life and to bind them together, to transform your future.

> **❝** If you want to *have* more, you must *be* more. To *be* more, you must *do* more.**❞**

Every decision you take and every great idea that you have begins as a spark in your mind. As you continue through this book, you will begin to capture these sparks. It only takes one to start a bushfire. It is almost incredible when you think about how much power you possess to change your life, simply by making a decision to change yourself.

You live best when you live by heart, head and hands. When you follow your heart's direction, your head is held high as you go about your business. Your hands are happily, effectively employed. Your heart sings as you move forward in life with an unstoppable momentum.

This book will teach you how to get your heart, head and hands working together. This trinity is the beginning of an exciting and fulfilling journey. The inner harmony created by this unity connects you with deep, positive emotions, providing inspiration and resourcefulness in all that you do. Now, through harnessing your own unique talents, you are free to express yourself fully to the world.

As the rope maker, each new day will be busy. You will need to commit all of your energy and creativity to the Golden Thread assignments that you will find throughout this book. Your hard work, character and values will determine the strength of your Golden Rope and the height to which you can climb.

With honesty, integrity, loyalty and love you can make your rope unbreakable.

Give yourself a head start

Condition yourself for new experiences and opportunities, and you will create a mindset that enables you to relaunch your life in an upward direction. Research shows that when you keep your mind stimulated, your brain function improves with time.

The power of your brain should never be underestimated. It is composed of billions of neurons – brain cells that communicate with one another – formed into connections and networks. Throughout your life, these connections and networks are shaped and developed according to your experiences. Scientists call this *plasticity*, after the Greek word for 'moulded'.

Living material is either growing or dying; there is no 'in-between' state. Your brain can grow new neurons up until the day you die – and it is never too late to expand your mind. As the rope maker, you must ensure that you put your brain to work. If you have a mindset that leaves you hungry for learning and for new experiences, you will get much more out of every aspect of your life.

66 A proactive attitude to change will lead to opportunities to change your life for the better. 99

The musician Frank Zappa summed it up perfectly when he said, 'The mind is like a parachute – it works only when it is open'. Exercise your mind regularly, and it will gain vitality and value.

It follows that if you are going to become the best that you can be, making the best Golden Rope that you can, your mind must be open – and must stay open. It must be ready to take on exciting – and sometimes nerve-racking – new ideas, challenges and goals. This simple principle is at the core of every Golden Thread that follows.

The right mindset brings with it so many possibilities. At 65 years old, I'm still learning. For me, a proactive attitude is closely associated with a general sense of well-being and purpose.

I'll admit that I wasn't always a model student. At school I often stared out of the window and daydreamed; teachers would throw board rubbers at me to get my attention. After leaving school I began working in one of the local mills, along with many of my peers. Life was grey in Bradford after the war, and it seemed to me that the course of my life had already been determined.

My nervous breakdown was a terrible low, but it also represented a new beginning. This negative experience left me with a keen interest in the mind's workings. My own mind had been my undoing; clearly, it was an extremely powerful tool. I reached the logical conclusion that if I could channel its output in a more positive direction my mind could be the making of me.

I was clever enough to realise that I wasn't clever enough. After all, the sum of the knowledge I had then had only taken me as far as a mill floor and a psychiatrist's office.

I would go on to co-found a chain of health clubs, after walking into a local gym and finding 'the thing that made my heart sing'. But it was my proactive attitude and my yearning to embark upon a steep learning curve that made it possible for me to even consider turning my dream into reality. When I stepped into that gym, everything about me changed in an instant – even the way I carried myself.

This same mindset has prevailed in my life ever since. When I took on my first employees, I engaged those who were la crème de la crème. I could measure myself against them, and I aimed to learn as much from them as I could.

Now that I am older, there is an expectation that I should stop or slow down. But why would I want to batten down the hatches now I've reached 65? As far as I'm concerned, when your mind begins to dull it's the beginning of the end. The story of my life isn't all told – not yet, anyway. Why would I want to stop, when I am enjoying myself? I feel that I have reached the halfway mark, and I am confident that the rest of my journey will be the best of my journey. It will be even more exhilarating than what has gone before.

Ready, steady, go!

You have already taken the first steps by buying this book and reading this far. Here are other actions and habits that will help you to exercise your mind and begin building your Golden Rope.

1. **Improve your posture**. This may be an unusual place to start, but studies have found that our emotions are closely linked to physical posture. You cannot separate the two: there are powerful links between feeling well and doing well. Researchers have discovered that when optimists are looking up, they perform better in tasks. Simply lifting your head can improve your mood.

Here's another reason to sit up straight: if you are slouched with your shoulders hunched forward, your lung capacity is restricted.

Oxygen fuels the brain; if you breathe shallowly, your intake of oxygen is reduced.

It takes relatively little effort to change your posture for the better, and the effects are instant. Not only will you feel more confident and energised, but people around you will regard you differently. When you walk like somebody who has a purpose, somewhere to go and aspirations in life, that is how you will be perceived by others – and yourself.

2. Check what you say to yourself. Edit your inner voice. Get into the habit of encouraging yourself. Be 'success conscious'. The ways in which we articulate our feelings to ourselves on a daily basis are crucial to our attitudes and emotions. If you tell yourself that you can or you cannot do something, you are right either way. Take 'can't' out of your everyday talk and thoughts and replace it with the question, 'How *can* I?' Ask yourself the right questions and your unconscious will come up with the right answers. You will move towards positive action and open up a bright new world of possibilities.

3. Smile at yourself. Always take your work seriously, but never take yourself seriously. Don't get wound up, even when you are criticised by others. Instead, take a deep breath and move on. Learn to smile at yourself; even when other people are amused at your expense, take their viewpoint. You want people to feel comfortable with you, and to be able to open up to you. If you are to develop and maintain good relationships, you need to keep people on your side.

4. Celebrate yourself. It's easy to get into the habit of putting ourselves down. Instead, get into the habit of casting modesty aside. All too often, when compliments are paid to us, rather than saying 'thank you' we shrug them off.

When you celebrate yourself and recognise your achievements, you lay the foundations for future success. Congratulate yourself out loud, and reward yourself regularly. Create your very own 'achievement file', as outlined in Chapter 2.

5. Good health. This subject will be covered more fully in Part 5 of this book: 'The Health Threads'. Good eating habits, good exercise and good rest have all been shown to enhance brain function, and will play an important role in your success.

6. Be responsive, rather than reactive. When patients take medicine, it is good if they 'respond' to that medicine and bad if they 'react' to it. The same goes for your approach to life. Don't allow others to ruin your day: 'respond' to events rather than 'react' to them, and make that extra effort to stay in control. If someone cuts you up in traffic, take a deep breath, relax and smile at them. It is often worth it, just to see their face!

Untangle the knots

You will find it easier to build your Golden Rope if you can keep your Golden Threads from becoming tangled, knotted or frayed by the following distractions:

o   **The television.** Be selective in your viewing. At the end of every programme that you watch, ask yourself: what did I just gain? Some programmes are informative and enlightening. Others, however, amount to little more than mind candy. It is often difficult to glean anything worthwhile from soap operas or daytime television. Instead, they offer viewers timetabled slots for dumbed-down escapism that numbs the mind. Why spend hours watching junk television, when you could be using that time to follow new interests or develop promising enterprises?

○ **Downmarket newspapers and magazines**. These are filled with negative news stories and nonsensical articles about vacuous celebrities. The benefits derived from reading these publications are, at best, minimal. Surely your time could be invested more wisely elsewhere?

○ **Lack of sleep**. Fatigue slows the brain and dampens any would-be sparks of inspiration. Get as much sleep as you need. If you are frequently worn out and operating on auto pilot, you cannot grow your mind. If you are so tired that you cannot get out of bed when your alarm clock goes off in the morning, you are off to a poor start. This is self-limiting behaviour.

○ **Gloomy outlooks**. The English language is littered with morose and energy-sapping phrases, such as 'I'm not bad' and 'I'm all right'. The subtext is: 'I'm surviving – but things could be better'. Really? If you could be better, why aren't you?

Monitor your own use of negative phrases. Work to eliminate them completely from your day-to-day conversations. When people ask how you are, tell them, 'I feel great'. It helps form the habit of positive conversation.

> ❝ 'I'm not bad' and 'I feel great': which of these two phrases do you think creates the best impression? ❞

Don't allow people – including yourself – to pigeonhole you or hold you back. You may find that the people around you want to keep you where you are. But unless they can see into the future, how can they possibly know what your future holds?

Don't take any notice of the know-it-alls. These are the 'backseat teachers' who are found perched by the pub door or hovering at the gym, dispensing half-baked advice to all and sundry. If they know so much, why are they *talking* instead of *doing*?

○ **Ageist attitudes**. Age is a self-imposed – and self-limiting – concept. When 102-year-olds have embraced Facebook and septuagenarians have made bids for the American presidency, what's your excuse? In truth, you're never too old to learn. In today's world the saying, 'You can't teach an old dog new tricks', just doesn't ring true anymore.

Welsh grandmother Rosie Swale-Pope, who is in her sixties, recently completed a five-year run around the globe. She was inspired to embark upon this solo adventure after her husband died of prostate cancer. The widow explained that his death had taught her 'more than anything about how precious life is, how short it can be, that you *have* to grab life, do what you can while you can, and try to give something back'. Her formidable mindset is an example to us all.

SUMMARY

○ It is up to you to take hold of the strands running through your life and to work them together to make your future. You are the rope maker.

○ If you are going to make the best Golden Rope that you can, and become the best that you can be, you must first prime your mind. Your actions and achievements are dictated by your attitude.

○ If you do not exercise your mind regularly, it will lose its vitality and value. A thirst for knowledge is created by passion and purpose.

ACTION POINTS

Every journey in life begins with those first steps. Here are three of yours.

1. Take up a new physical activity. This could be anything, from walking to work to trapeze lessons. The choice is yours.

2. Plan a television-free day every week. Fill the time with another interest. If it is possible, this will include your family.

3. If you don't already have a place for your books, make one. Keep them all in one place, in a bookcase or on a designated shelf. If possible, keep them in a home office or have a 'creative corner' of the house where you can go. With your own reference library, you will be able to access things quickly. Order your computer files and folders in the same way.

W O R K S H E E T

You are currently sat here reading this book – but how are you sat? Look at yourself: are you sitting upright, or are you slumped? Is your chin up or down? Are you alert or do you feel that at any given moment you could fall asleep?

Change your posture right now and tick off the improvements as you make them.

a. Raise your chin. Look up at the ceiling. ☐
b. Snuggle your spine into the back of your chair. ☐
c. Roll your shoulders back. ☐
d. Sit with your upper legs at 90 degrees to your body. ☐
e. Press your feet flat against the ground. ☐
f. Take a deep breath. Hold it for five seconds and exhale. Repeat twice. ☐

This may seem like a simple exercise – and it is, but the actions that can improve your life for the better and take you in the directions that you want to go are often as simple as they are efficient.

PART

1

The Learning Threads

CHAPTER

In praise of learning

One of the great motivational speakers, Zig Ziglar, sums it up perfectly when he says, 'If you carry on doing what you've been doing, you'll carry on getting what you've been getting'. In other words you cannot change your future by staying as you are; it is futile even to try.

Now, as a newly fledged rope maker, you must embrace change. You are now ready to embark upon a learning curve. When you take away as much as you can from your actions, experiences and opportunities, you head for the sky, growing and strengthening your Golden Threads all the while.

What is learning?

Learning isn't restricted to schools and universities, but is a continuous, lifelong process: hence the saying, 'the University of Life'.

If you intend to fulfil your potential and become the best that you can possibly be, a never-ending search for knowledge must become one of your primary values.

❝ Everything you need to know to change your life is out there somewhere. All you have to do is find it.❞

The knowledge you seek, which will inform and enhance the Golden Threads in your life, may be found in printed guides or on talking books. You may find it at your local library or on websites. You may find it when people come into your life at opportune times. It will begin to appear when you begin asking the right questions; when people help you by sharing the sums of their knowledge and experiences.

Map your route

Inspiration creates energy and a hunger to learn, so if you have found 'the thing that makes your heart sing', you have given yourself a great head start. At this stage, you will fall into one of two camps. You may have identified set goals to work towards. These could range from setting up your own business in a specific industry or sector, to becoming a better parent or partner.

If you fit this description, you should be able to answer the following questions:

1. What do I want?
2. Why do I want it?
3. When do I want it?
4. What action can I take now?

On the other hand, you may be unsure about what you want out of life. Maybe, like us, you may have followed a direction that has led you to a dead end. Perhaps you are unsure where your talents lie. Perhaps you are seeking something that you have yet to identify, which remains tantalisingly out of reach.

Try this simple exercise.

Turn off your mobile, unplug your telephone, switch off the TV and radio and sit quietly. Now imagine your perfect working day or weekday.

What would your perfect working day look like? How would it begin? What would you be doing? What would make your heart sing, put your head in gear and set your hands to work? Would you be working at home, or would you be working away? Would you be in the UK? Would you be in another country? Would it involve travel? Would it involve your own business? Who and what would feature in it? How would you feel when your perfect day ended? Grab a pen and write it all down on the page provided; it will help you to understand better what it is that you seek.

My perfect working day

If you find it difficult to imagine your perfect day, have the confidence to keep asking yourself the above questions. Eventually your unconscious mind will give in and tell you the right answers. Inspiration will come. Remember: if you don't know what you are looking for, you won't find it by doing nothing. You can sit around like a lump and wait for inspiration to come knocking on your door

– but what if it doesn't turn up? You will serve yourself better by going out to look for it.

It is often the case that the greatest challenges lead to the best results. Take Cavanacaw in Northern Ireland, which is the UK's largest goldmine. There, the gold doesn't just pop to the surface in handy chunks and nuggets, while the workers sit around eating bacon butties. The precious metal is buried deep in the earth. Its particles are so small, they aren't visible to the naked eye. To find the gold, the workers have had to dig thousands of tons of earth out of a large open pit that now stretches across four acres of peat bog. But find the gold they have: the mine at Cavanacaw turns a good profit, yielding 30,000 ounces every year.

❝ If you are to strike gold, be prepared to dig deep and get dirt beneath your fingernails. ❞

Many people, perhaps yourself included, leave things until they become critical before they are spurred into action. I waited until I had a nervous breakdown aged 20, but I discovered that for all of us, adversity provides the seeds to equal or greater opportunities. It is down to us to find those seeds of opportunity and cultivate them. For me, the subsequent period of intensive learning meant that, for the first time, I was impelled to plan an exciting future.

Following the breakdown, I spent a lot of time in bed and my doctor recommended a change of job. After the amount of sleep I had been getting, I thought that a job as a tester for the local bed factory would be ideal! But I took an office-based role at an engineering firm, as a stop-gap. At around the same time I began developing a passion for weight training and keep-fit, which helped me to work off tension and brought about dramatic improvements in my health. As my state of mind improved over the next two years, I began to ponder what I wanted to do with my life. I didn't want to stay in my office role and I didn't want to repeat the bitter experiences of my past. These concerns inspired me to embark on a steep learning curve. I was determined to take my life in a forward direction. But where — and how?

One afternoon at work, with all my jobs for the day completed, I spotted the Yellow Pages telephone directory. This gave me an idea. I decided to look at all the local businesses in the directory, to see if I could gain inspiration for my future from any of them. This was a simple action, but it was to have a profound effect on my life.

As I turned each page and studied each listing, one advertisement caught my eye. It was for a new fitness centre just 30 minutes' drive from my home. This was in 1966, when health clubs were in their infancy; at the time, I worked out in a wooden hut filled with loose weights and benches. When I read about this fitness centre's innovative facilities, with its showers, sauna, coffee lounge and state-of-the-art equipment, I had a 'eureka' moment. I was gripped. I had the conviction that this was where my future lay, and I was determined to make it happen. It was the most wonderful feeling, one that I will always remember. I had found my purpose in life. There and then, I began planning my future.

My first step was to join as a member of the club. This was a period of intensive learning, which gave me time to check out the facilities, learn the ropes, network with the team and get to know the management. I got my hands on all the fitness books that I could find; I began subscribing to various American bodybuilding magazines. As I learned more and more, my enthusiasm continued to grow. I was determined to expand my knowledge, so I began asking questions of instructors and fellow members at the club. I quizzed them about techniques, and new or unfamiliar exercises. I learned what to do, and I soon saw the benefits. My appearance became more muscular, I slept well at night and I felt great when I woke up in the morning. Gaining confidence in my own views, I went from being an amateur with an interest in weight-training to a respected source of information and advice.

Six months after joining the club, I became a gym instructor there. I would go on to co-found a chain of health clubs in the north of England.

Flicking through the Yellow Pages that afternoon, I had discovered that the part of the brain that deals with creativity is fuelled and driven by emotion. In this way, a single spark of inspiration changed my life. A single spark can light up your whole world.

Of course, flicking through the Yellow Pages won't work for everyone! But my simple search changed everything for me. When you are looking for a new path and a better life, you have to start somewhere. Today we have the internet, which gives us the world at our fingertips. Why not begin there?

Take the first steps

Have you noticed how people rarely enjoy personal and professional development courses at work when they are forced to go on them? They don't gain maximum value from these learning experiences, because they didn't really want to be there in the first place. Don't let yourself fall into this trap. Instead, learn at your own pace. If you are able to identify and focus upon what interests you most, your learning will stimulate you and encourage creative thinking.

Even the smallest of actions, which may not seem life changing or even important at the time, will help you to grow. Set aside time for reading. In every situation, conversation, relationship, book or news article, be on the lookout for something that will spark or strengthen a Learning Thread in your life. Develop an eagle eye for opportunities when you are out and about. Ideas could come from anywhere: from a slogan emblazoned across the side of a van, from the shop front for a newly opened business, or from online networks and forums.

Whenever you encounter a difficult question or an unfamiliar situation, find the courage to admit that you don't know the answer and ask someone to help you. This may feel uncomfortable at first, because from an early age we are conditioned not to draw attention to ourselves, or to put our heads above the parapet. However, an inquisitive nature will put you ahead of the game. Get over the embarrassment.

> 66 Ask the question, and you're a fool for a minute; don't ask the question, and you're a fool for life. 99

At the end of every day, sit down and review what you have gained *from* that day, rather than how you got through it. Carry out your own review: what did you learn? Remember, 'I have learned nothing' is the wrong answer.

The achievement file

When Marc took the decision to steer his life in a different direction he began to compile an achievement file. Since then, he's filled it with everything, from yellowed scraps of notepaper to magazine cuttings. Each item represents a personal high. The file is a prop and an inspiration to his ambitions and sense of self-worth. When he started to compile his file, it was filled with small items; back then, he could have fitted his achievements on to the back of a postage stamp.

Over the years the file has grown, and whenever he's feeling negative, or that he's stagnating, he pulls it out of his desk drawer and looks through it. He then feels a renewed sense of pride in his achievements and, without fail, his motivation to learn and strive for self-improvement receives a terrific boost. Keeping a file like this is addictive: once it's there, you want to keep adding to it.

Here are five items from his achievement file.

Marc

1.   These are two items really, but they go together. The first is my dismal school report from 1975. It reads, 'has not done himself justice'.

The second item is a certificate from MENSA, dated 1992, stating that my IQ places me in the top 2 per cent of the population. I keep these items because they show what I can do, when I apply myself.

2.   A pile of letters from former clients, dated 1984. This would have been shortly after I met Barry and began working as a manager in one of his health clubs. The written comments include, 'friendly and considerate', 'very reliable and knowledgeable' and 'always smart in appearance and courteous to all members'. These are in my achievement file because they represent recognition of my hard work. When somebody takes the trouble to thank you for what you have done for them, it makes you feel good.

3.   A Father's Day card from my eldest son. This dates from the early 1990s: he had gone to a great deal of effort to form the wobbly letters that spell his name. Every time I look at this card I feel happy; to be a parent is an achievement in itself.

4.   A glossy colour leaflet, promoting a presentation I gave in Mauritius in 2002. I was invited to talk about goal-setting to 250 top business achievers from South Africa. This is in my

achievement file because it was a memorable event, and I was so proud to have been invited to speak there. When I look at my name and photograph on this leaflet, it hits home just how far I have come.

5. A stack of leaving cards, given to me by team members in 2008. These marked my departure from a telecommunications company that I had sold the year previously. The messages include, 'I've learned tons from you over the years. I'm grateful that you believed in me', and 'Your words and guidance have meant a lot to me and helped me to mature into the person that I am today.' I keep these cards in the file because they demonstrate that I have made a positive difference to people's lives. To my mind, this is one of my greatest achievements.

SUMMARY

● By extracting the maximum value from your actions, experiences and opportunities, and seeking benefits from every situation, you will add new threads to your Golden Rope.

● Everything you need to know to change your life is out there somewhere – you just have to find it.

● Even the smallest of actions, which may not seem life changing or even important at the time, can create or strengthen a Learning Thread in your life.

ACTION POINTS

1. Get into the habit of active listening. Our ears never stop growing, even when we are old – perhaps there's a message there! The more space you give people so that they can talk, the more you can learn from them.

2. Travel time should be life time, not dead time: replace those CDs in your glove compartment or fill that space on your mp3 player with personal development CDs or talking books. For a selection of good CDs and talking books, visit our website at www.yourgoldenthreads.com.

3. Spend a couple of hours looking back over your life and creating an achievement file of your own. Keep the file within easy reach. Every single item that you place inside it should make you feel proud of yourself. It could include photographs of your family, certificates, letters and clippings. Pick it up for a 'pick me up'.

WORKSHEET

List five of the items that you have placed or are planning to place into your achievement file. Explain briefly why they are there.

Item . . . .

Why? . . . .

. . . .

Item . . . .

Why? . . . .

. . . .

Item ....

Why? ....
....

Item ....

Why? ....
....

Item ....

Why? ....
....

CHAPTER 3

How to become a knowledge glutton

I can't and won't stop learning. Whenever I meet someone who has something admirable about them, I like to ask lots of questions – usually quickly, before they escape!

After I hit rock bottom in my early thirties, I adopted a scattergun approach to learning. I went on every personal development course I could find, played CDs in my car, read lots of useful books and joined all the organisations and clubs that interested me. I adopted a trial-and-error approach and it wasn't the quickest way out of my situation, but in the end it worked for me. These ranged from Toastmasters, which develops public speaking and leadership skills, to network marketing companies, where I learned sales and business skills.

After meeting lots of new people and discovering a good deal about myself, I found that opportunities began to trickle through. This was how I came to set up a telecommunications company, despite being a relative newcomer to that industry. I learned what was happening in that market and discovered that a space needed filling. Once again, I was stepping into the unknown. In the early years I made a number of poor judgements and costly mistakes, but I always learned from them. In August 2000 I put all that hard-won learning to use when I set up a second telecommunications company, which was profitable from the word go.

Six Honest Serving Men

Six Honest Serving Men is a wonderful poem by Rudyard Kipling. It has become very popular among motivational speakers and executive coaches, because it pinpoints the essence of successful learning and development. It begins:

I keep six honest serving-men
(They taught me all I knew);
Their names are What and Why and When
And How and Where and Who.

Cultivating an inquisitive attitude is a principle that will serve you throughout your life. Opinions are like noses: everyone has one, but they are all different. Ask lots of questions, and you'll receive lots of answers. As most people like talking about themselves, this isn't difficult to do.

- 'What do you do?'
- 'Who did you learn from?'
- 'When did you realise?'
- 'Where can I get that?'
- 'How long did it take you?'
- 'Why did you do that?'

Note their answers and aim to learn something from every conversation. If you get into the habit of sending your *Six Honest Serving Men* out to work – and throughout this book and beyond, you are encouraged to do so – you will be able to boost your learning and skills, while making the most of opportunities that present themselves.

Your next steps

1. Expand your comfort zone. Or at the very least, don't be afraid to do so. Just because something is new, untried or ambitious, why place it beyond your reach? It can often be that the most nerve-racking experiences or situations are the most valuable in the long term. Stretch yourself.

As adults, we come with a ready-made roster of values and beliefs. Some of them are drawn from our personal experiences;

others have been hoovered up from family, friends and our social backgrounds. Some of them are sound; others, however, may be soaked in inertia. They can include the conviction that you will never achieve beyond a certain point, or above a certain level. Such beliefs will only hold you back; glass ceilings were made to be smashed.

Our values and beliefs guide our decisions and give meaning to our lives. Even when this guidance may operate at an unconscious level, it has a powerful role in shaping our lives and our futures.

As a boy I used to cycle to Ilkley with friends to fish in the River Wharfe. I was always uplifted when we went out of the grey city and into the countryside, with its beautiful scenery and big houses. I would be downcast when we returned to the grime and muck of Bradford, and I was determined that when I grew up I would escape it.

I gained the nickname 'Johnny Opposite', because I often queried what I was told. I was given this name by the father of a friend, a man who owned a small piggery, after he spelled out my future prospects as he saw them. I found his vision to be limiting and depressing, and told him so. When he began calling me 'Johnny Opposite', I felt that I didn't fit in. At the time, it was horribly embarrassing. Now I look back and I am pleased that even then I was prepared to take myself out of my comfort zone and away from what I knew. I'm a better person for it.

2. Form your own opinions. Do so even if you prefer to keep them to yourself. Question everything that you know; again, this returns to the idea that you have much to gain when you step outside your comfort zone. Read widely and give yourself the time and space in which to think. Inform and clarify your views on events and issues.

3. Become a researcher. Improve your communication and comprehension skills by learning a couple of new words every week. If you do not own a dictionary, invest in one or save an online dictionary to your Favourites folder. Refer to it whenever you hear a word that you do not know. Whenever something or someone piques your interest, research that thing or person online or offline, to find out as much as you can.

66 Develop a hunger for knowledge – and feed it regularly. 99

4. Leisure time is learning time. When you are extremely selective about your television viewing, it makes sense to extract as much as you can from the programmes that you do continue to watch. Documentaries and arts programmes can be inspiring and informative. They may even provide you with new ideas about where you want to go and what you want to be. A word, phrase or picture can be all it takes to get you thinking and making fresh plans.

5. Spend time with those you admire. You may admire their professional success; you may admire their talent for forming new friendships; you may admire something else altogether. Make an effort to spend time with these people and get to know them better. Learn from them, and put your new skills to good use.

Later on in this book, in the Relationship Threads section, we will explore this step in greater detail and describe the benefits of having a personal or professional 'mentor' in your life. The chances are that wherever you are in your life, someone has been there before you. That person is your perfect mentor. They are living, breathing proof that your ambitions can be achieved.

Failure as a learning tool

Life has its ups and downs, but here in the UK we have a terrible attitude to failure. There is still a great stigma attached to setbacks such as going out of business, getting divorced, losing money or being made redundant. Sadly, this means that we often translate simple setbacks into crushing defeats.

Contrast this attitude to that in other countries such as America. There, business mistakes, bankruptcies and failures are viewed as rites of passage for entrepreneurs and others who seek to succeed.

If and when you confront failure, it may help you to remember that some of the world's most successful men and women have hit bottom and bounced back.

○ **Johnny Cash** became the youngest star to be inducted into the Country Music Hall of Fame in 1980, but 12 years later Johnny Cash's music career had slid into the doldrums. His records weren't selling and he had parted ways with one record company after another. Cash refused to give up. He inked a deal with a label better known for rap and hard rock music, and recorded an album in his living room. It was a surprise success: sales took off and the album won a Grammy. A decade of hit records and industry accolades followed.

○ **Laura Ashley**, the British designer and mother of four, began printing Victorian-style headscarves in 1953; several high street stores placed orders, and staff members were employed to handle the growing sales. However, her young company suffered disaster in 1958, after a river close to its premises flooded its banks. Fabrics, dyes and expensive new equipment were all found ruined, floating in three feet of water. Undaunted, Laura Ashley and her husband redoubled their efforts to create a successful business while raising their young family. Piece by piece, they rebuilt the business and clawed back all that they had lost. Times were hard, with every spare penny plunged back into the company and a number of new lines launched, but their efforts paid off. By 1960, Laura Ashley's annual turnover had quadrupled.

o Walt Disney, the famous animator, founded his first company in Kansas City when he was just 20, but went bankrupt two years later after his investors pulled out. He left for Hollywood with everything he owned: a few items of clothing and some salvaged drawing materials. The rest is history.

You cannot see into the future or know what lies around the corner, but what you can do is develop a resilient attitude that will stand you in good stead for all your tomorrows.

If you do not fear failure, you will be more willing to experiment with new ideas and you will not be afraid to embrace unfamiliar and exciting opportunities. If you refuse to let life's knocks keep you from springing back up again, you will learn a lot more. In time, you will reap the benefits.

Failure is not an outcome but an attitude. As Winston Churchill noted, 'Success is going from failure to failure without loss of enthusiasm'.

Today's professional sportspeople get to where they are because they endure millions of failures. They experiment with different shots, different balls, different jumps and different ideas, until they find the shots, balls and ideas that win. Think of failure as a long-term investment in yourself, and remember: nothing learned, nothing gained.

When my business failed in 1990, people came to our house to offer their sympathies. They spoke in low, hushed tones, as if they were attending a funeral.

This attitude bewildered me. I was very disappointed, but I wasn't devastated. By this time, the Golden Threads running through my life included my wife, family and friends. I had attended many different courses and studied hard; my sense of self and my self-confidence were much improved. Because my Golden Rope was thick and strong, I was able to hold on to it and pull myself up again.

New opportunities were not long in coming, and I couldn't wait to get started again. I looked around and learned to value what I had, rather than what I had lost. I also learned some very important business lessons, which have stood me in good stead ever since.

The signs of successful learning

As you fill your mind with new opportunities, actions and experiences, you will sense the beginnings of a transformation. In everyday life you will notice a new buzz and energy. When you wake up in the morning, you will get out of bed because you *want* to, not because you have to. Your life will take on a new meaning. Your hunger for learning will continue to grow, until you are constantly craving new information and ideas.

When you pull on an elastic band it will stretch and stretch until, finally, it has stretched so far that it cannot return to its previous shape. Learning has an identical effect upon the mind: keep expanding it and, after a while, you will have progressed so far that there will be no going back.

66 A fleeting moment of inspiration can alter your destiny forever. 99

The guitar-maker Learning Threads

Jim Fleeting, an award-winning Yorkshire guitar-maker, shows what can be achieved if these learning principles are followed.

Jim used to work in IT in London but, although the pay and the hours were good, he wasn't fulfilled and he didn't know what he wanted to do with his life. The prospect of sitting behind his plastic grey office desk, day in and day out until retirement, horrified him. In his spare time, he played the bass and guitar.

In 2004, when he was 27, Jim and a friend visited Spain's Basque region for a cycling holiday in the mountains. As they rode up one particularly steep mountainside, little did Jim know that by the time they came down the other side, his life would have changed forever.

The path was rugged and treacherous; it soared above them and seemed to go on forever. They pressed on for hours before collapsing, exhausted and sweating, on an unusually flat area of turf miles from the nearest village. As they gathered their breath beneath the hot afternoon sun, Jim looked around and realised that they were lying on a neatly laid out football pitch. The grass was clipped, the sections had been carefully marked and goalposts were propped up at both ends. Gradually he understood: the villagers loved football so much that even the remote, rocky location would not keep them from playing their favourite game. They had sought out and levelled the only flat area on their mountain, and turned it into an immaculate pitch. Jim was impressed and sat there, admiring the villagers' handiwork.

66 It dawned on him that if you wanted something badly enough – even if what you wanted dwarfed your reasonable expectations – you would find a way of getting it. 99

He explained this to his friend. They fell to talking about their own ambitions, and the pair began to send their *Six Honest Serving Men* out to work.

'I've always wanted to build my own guitar', Jim said. '**When** I was a teenager, learning to play, I saw a cross-section diagram of an acoustic guitar and I thought it was the most wonderful thing I had ever seen.'

'If these villagers can make this mountainside into their football pitch', his friend replied, '**why** couldn't you make a guitar?'

Jim thought about for this for a while. 'I could get an instruction book – but I don't have the money for the tools. **Where** could I get that from? I'd have to spend years saving.'

'So don't buy them,' said his friend. '**Go** to an evening class – there must be one somewhere!'

Inspiration had struck. When Jim returned to London a week later, he was full of energy and couldn't wait to begin learning. He finally found an evening course on the other side of the city. There, he learned to build his first guitar. Throwing himself into his work, he emerged top of his class. His instructors were impressed with his enthusiasm and talent, and encouraged him to develop his potential further.

Jim was already creating his own Golden Rope, and he seized every chance to reach out and secure new opportunities and experiences that would help him on his climb. Now that he had found his calling, his ambitions multiplied along with his guitar-making skills. He decided to make a career out of building musical instruments and wrote to his favourite bass-maker, a Pennsylvania craftsman called Ken Smith, asking to be taken on as an apprentice. Ken Smith replied, explaining that he only employed those who had graduated from a prestigious guitar-building school in the Arizona desert.

Undeterred, Jim applied to the guitar-building school, and won a place. He left his office job, sunk his savings into tuition costs and set off. In Arizona, he worked and studied around the clock. His teachers asked him to join them as an assistant instructor. But Jim reached out and sought another, better opportunity.

At a guitar trade show in California, Jim heard a fellow English accent in the crowd. He tracked down that accent's owner, and the two men began talking. The talk turned into a drink, and the drink became a dinner. The man was a Yorkshire entrepreneur with a chain of successful music stores. He said that if Jim returned to England, Jim could set up his guitar-making business and workshop in one of those stores. The pair shook hands.

Just four years later, Jim Fleeting Guitars has already outgrown that original workshop and now occupies stand-alone premises in North Yorkshire. Its reputation for high-quality craftsmanship has spread, and Jim receives a steady stream of orders for his custom-built instruments. His achievements have been featured in *Guitar* and *Guitarist* magazines, and his clients include several high-profile musicians.

Even though Jim has found what makes his heart sing, he still works hard to push the boundaries of his learning higher and higher still. In 2008 he won a scholarship to return to America to study with Ervin Somogyi, a guitar-maker regarded as one of the best in the world.

Jim's quest for learning began with a cycle ride up a mountainside. He's still aiming for the summit.

❝ If you want something badly enough – even if what you want dwarfs your reasonable expectations – you will find a way of getting it. ❞

SUMMARY

● Keep learning and, after a while, you will find there is no going back. As you fill your mind with new opportunities, actions and experiences, you will sense the beginnings of a transformation.

● Keep asking the right questions of yourself and of those around you, and you will alight upon the right answers.

● Turn failure to your advantage. Learn from it, and think of it as a long-term investment in yourself.

ACTION POINTS

1. Don't let the fear of failure hold you back: go the extra mile and confront your fears. If you don't like talking to groups, or being the centre of attention, join a public-speaking organisation or make a point of talking and asking questions in group situations. Fear knocks at the door – but answer and there will be nobody there.

2. Carry a small notepad or blank cards around with you. Keep them in your bag, or in your pocket. Whenever inspiration strikes, be it an idea for a new business or the phone number of a new contact, jot it down. It could be the opportunity that changes your life.

3. Set up Google Alerts on subjects that interest you. You will be able to access a vast array of opinions on different subjects. Those who are unfamiliar with Google Alerts should visit www.google.com/alerts. There, enter your e-mail address and keywords for the subjects that interest you. Whenever an article featuring one or more of those words is published online, a link to the article will be automatically e-mailed to you.

WORKSHEET

Keep the next page bookmarked, and fill out a learning diary every day for the next two weeks. List your experiences and 'learns' and rate them on a scale of 1 to 10, according to the value that you feel you have extracted from them. A life-changing experience should be marked as 10 – but remember, even the smallest learning experiences count. We've given a few examples to help get you started.

At the end of two weeks, read your entries back to yourself. You may well discover that during this short period of time you have learned a surprising amount.

Example

EXPERIENCE

Got talking to a HR Manager at the gym

Listened to a CD about goal-setting

Booked and attended meeting with bank manager

EXPERIENCE

WHAT YOU HAVE LEARNED FROM IT	VALUE (1–10)
Vacant position in her organisation	
Encouraged me to apply	8
Want to start a family in the next three years	9
How to avoid unnecessary charges	5

WHAT YOU HAVE LEARNED FROM IT	VALUE (1–10)

EXPERIENCE

WHAT YOU HAVE LEARNED FROM IT	VALUE (1–10)

PART 2

The Career Threads

CHAPTER 4

Are you where you want to be?

'**S**o, what do you *do* then?'

    When meeting people for the first time, you have probably been asked this question. It is a dreary ice-breaker, but it goes to show that – whether you like it or not – your career choices define you.

    Everyone has Career Threads, from high-flying business executives to those featured on the Civil List. Career Threads feed, clothe and shelter you and your loved ones. They get you up in the morning, keep you up late at night and are reasons for being, doing and having.

    Your Career Threads furnish you with a strong sense of purpose, propel you onwards and are woven tightly with the other threads in your Golden Rope. Your Wealth Threads are closely bound to them. Your Family Threads are nourished by them. If your work is 'the thing that makes your heart sing', strong Career Threads will enrich and strengthen your Spiritual Threads too.

    Even the poet Philip Larkin, who described his work – albeit affectionately – as an *old toad*, wouldn't have been without it. In his poem 'Toads Revisited', he noted that a day in the park *Should feel better than work*, but went on to argue that jobless men were *stupid and weak*:

Turning over their failures
By some bed of lobelias,
Nowhere to go but indoors
Nor friends but empty chairs –

He concluded that work, by driving our lives forward, is at the very core of our identities.

When I was out of work, inertia quickly set in. I sometimes had to force myself to get out of bed in the morning, because there didn't seem to be much point in getting up. After all, what reasons did I have? I had no prospects – or so I thought – no career and nothing to drive me onwards. Benefits were paid directly into my bank account, so I didn't even have to go and collect them.

With the inertia came numbness. It was as if my brain had shifted into a neutral gear. I had little to contribute to other people's conversations; there is only so much to be said about daytime television. Fortunately I was able to snap out of this state of mind, but I am keenly aware that apathy is an easy habit to get into – and a difficult one to break. It was as if the real me had been driven away. Apathy settled upon me like a slow, creeping disease.

After I discovered the career that became an important part of my life, everything changed. All of a sudden I was building a team that was dependent upon me. I had to give presentations, and had to set the bar when it came to sales. I was focused and stimulated by the presence of like-minded individuals around me. My drive to succeed was stronger than ever.

My company didn't make any money at first, but it was what it made of me that mattered. There is a great sense of purpose that comes from creating and building.

Dead ends and roadblocks

Why is it that if work is so important to us, a BBC poll found that 35 per cent of workers 'hate' their jobs? British workers put in some of the longest hours in Europe – 41.4 hours a week, on average – and have relatively little time off. Yet it appears that millions of us are stuck in jobs or careers that we do not enjoy. If you don't find your work rewarding, you are wasting a large chunk of your life that you are never going to get back.

There are many reasons why people allow themselves to become mired in jobs that they do not like.

○   **The line of least resistance** is an easy path to follow – but may lead nowhere. Those who have low self-esteem and weak Spiritual Threads lack the confidence to attempt new challenges. They create a ripple effect: they won't try this or they couldn't possibly do that, and so on. Because they don't feel able to step outside their comfort zones, they make up excuses and stick to what they know. They stay where they are, rooted to the same spot, crippled by their lack of self-belief. If you are ever feeling low, or racked with self-doubt, revisit the Spiritual Threads section of this book and repeat the exercises at the end of the chapters.

○   Employers have reported that many people – particularly today's school and university leavers – come equipped with a **sense of entitlement**. They want promotions and pay rises sooner rather than later, before they have proved themselves and their value. If they are denied these benefits, they become frustrated and unhappy. People place their 'want' and their 'have' before their 'be' and 'do'. If this sounds like you, work hard to justify your expectations and demands.

❝ Do more than you are paid to do so that, someday, you will get paid more for what you do. ❞

○   When things aren't going well, many people tend to point the finger and apportion **blame**. They blame anything and anyone, from computers to public transport to those around them. In the long run, it's wiser to take responsibility for your own situation, so that you are better placed to bring about change.

❝ Responsibility = to respond with ability. ❞

○   Lots of people **fly out of the education chute and fall into the nearest job or career** without much planning or consideration. Instead, they make the best of the situation in which they find themselves. Some of them do extremely well, making a lot of money. However, over time people change. Years down the line, they may find that the jobs they fell into aren't for them after all. The good news is that there are always opportunities out there for those willing and able to seize them. Grow bigger than the job you are in, and those chances of promotion are greatly increased.

o Those who **take on responsibilities** such as mortgages, expensive cars and families often feel obliged to devote themselves to work they dislike, if it means they can maintain their chosen lifestyles and strive for financial security. They are shackled to their incomes; like slaves on Roman warships, they have no choice but to keep rowing.

o **Poor finances** tie many people to unfulfilling jobs when they would rather be elsewhere. It has been said that 'job' stands for 'Just Over Broke': a job is a means to an end, whereas a career is longer-term and much more substantial. Unfortunately, those who have no savings, live hand to mouth and always have 'too much month at the end of the money' are often hard-pressed to make the transition from a job to a new career. Even training packages, which would propel them upwards, take up resources that they don't have. If this is you, read the Wealth Threads section of this book, which describes how you can get money – and how you can keep it.

o Older people may feel that they have **left it too late** to begin again. But are they right – or are they holding themselves back?

You are always 'the right age' to make a fresh start. I should know: at 65, I have a number of exciting work projects on the go. I enjoy reinventing myself and marking new achievements. New opportunities energise and motivate me. I propel myself forward – I don't have to be pushed.

I am surrounded by friends and retirees who are convinced that our age group is 'past it'. Some people are surprised by how busy I am, because they feel that I should be 'slowing down'. These attitudes bewilder me, but I do understand how they have come about. Society conditions us to retire from life, as well as work, when we reach our sixties. It expects us to join the 'dressing gown and slippers' brigade. We are encouraged to look forward to our retirement years – as if everything that goes before is tiring and unpleasant!

The way I see it, if somebody has looked forward to retirement, that person must have had a miserable working life. What's to admire about that? What a tragic waste of time and talent.

I have also found that as most people get older they become afraid of the consequences of breaking out and doing something different. They feel that their time for action has passed, and that it is too late to change the direction in which their lives are headed. Instead of breaking through ceilings at work, they lower them.

This saddens me, because it simply isn't true that career options tail off with age. Although I won't deny that age discrimination still exists, there are plenty of opportunities out there. Certain employers, such as B&Q, actively recruit older people to their workforce. Alternatively, why not start your own business?

Lots of well-known, successful people didn't even start out until relatively late in life. The Pulitzer Prize–winning author Annie Proulx didn't write her first novel until she was in her late fifties. Winston Churchill was in his sixties when he became Prime Minister. The successful American artist Grandma Moses didn't embark upon her painting career until she was in her seventies, after abandoning a previous career in embroidery because of arthritis.

Why them and not us? As a long-time entrepreneur, I am currently involved with three different enterprises. There is so much more that I plan to do. Let's face it: I'm simply not ready to see out the rest of my days sitting in my conservatory, drinking tea and doing Sudoku!

● For some people, a wretched working life is offset by a fulfilling or luxury-laden life outside the workplace. Change and self-improvement aren't for everyone: if you are only motivated by money and material possessions, it makes sense to focus on flashing pound signs rather than the nitty-gritty of your working day.

Because you are reading this book, the chances are that you want more than this. You don't wish to leave your talents unspent – and for the majority of us, life is simply too short for a miserable job. Because work is central to your well-being, a Golden Rope without strong Career Threads is incomplete.

Sadly, if you keep doing work that makes you miserable, your work performance and your family life may suffer. Then, when you receive negative feedback or fail to get promoted, you will become more miserable still and your Career Threads will begin to erode.

Which would you rather have: well-paid work that you don't enjoy, or work that pays less but is stimulating and rewarding? Give this decision plenty of thought. It's an important question to ask yourself, because your values shape you.

66 Make your plans and don't settle for less than you deserve. 99

You know you're in the wrong line of work when ...

1. Every Sunday night, you get the Monday morning feeling. When you think about the coming week's work, your heart sinks and you become tense and anxious.
2. You don't want to get out of bed in the mornings. You press the snooze button and roll over.
3. When you get to work, you begin clock-watching. Time passes slowly: when you look up at the clock, only five minutes have passed.
4. You fritter away your time at work. You don't think your best thoughts, make your best plans or carry out your best actions. Instead, you wander off to get a cup of tea, or to join the office gossip around the water cooler.
5. By the time you get home, your day has put you in an irritable mood. All you want to do is pour yourself a drink and watch the television.
6. You don't believe in what you are selling, making or doing. You daydream at work, and you are often struck by the thought that you could be doing something better.

You know you're in the right line of work when ...

1. You don't mind getting out of bed in the mornings. You don't hit the snooze button. You leave the house with a spring in your step.
2. You think your best thoughts, make your best plans and carry out your best actions. It comes naturally to you.
3. You feel fulfilled. You have an optimistic attitude towards life in general.
4. You often catch yourself looking forward to and planning your next day. You like to plan your work, and work your plan.
5. Even when you are not at work, you are happy to 'talk shop', or to plough through work-related ideas in your mind.
6. At the end of the day you are tired, but it is a happy tired. You feel pleased and sleepy, rather than drained and fatigued.

Live to work

If your present work does not fulfil you and you are considering a fresh start, you are not alone. In recent decades, working life has been transformed. It used to be that jobs were for life; these days, people change careers every five years or so. They re-educate themselves, reinvent themselves and venture forth.

Whatever you decide to do, don't rush into anything. Before you hand in your notice or hang up your work clothes, think long and hard. Your exit must be planned, and timing is everything. If you have no savings and your current job pays the bills, read the Wealth Threads section and save a contingency fund before you throw everything up in the air. If unemployment figures are soaring, don't leave one job before you have a new workplace or career plan lined up and ready to go.

If and when you are in a position to move on, grab the opportunity with both hands. Keep your eyes and ears open, use your network of Relationship Threads to find out about any openings, and begin focusing upon the future rather than the present. Paint a beautiful horizon and set your sail towards it.

Once you know what you want to do or be, you have given yourself a valuable head start. In the next chapter, 'The Career Guideposts', you will learn about various strategies and actions to help you carve a rewarding new career out of 'the thing that makes your heart sing'.

SUMMARY

o   Good Career Threads furnish you with a strong sense of purpose, drive your life forward and form a core part of your identity.

o   Career Threads are woven tightly into your Golden Rope. They enrich and strengthen your other Golden Threads.

○ Millions of us have been in or are stuck in jobs or careers that we do not enjoy – but if you don't find your work rewarding, that's a large chunk of life that you aren't going to get back.

○ There are many reasons why people allow themselves to become mired in jobs that they do not like. Inertia is one of the most common.

○ If you wish to embark upon a new career, planning and preparation are key. Turn your focus away from your present, and train your thoughts upon what you would like your future to be.

ACTION POINTS

Consider your current job or career, then read the following statements and give yourself marks on a sliding scale from 0 to 10. A score of 0 indicates that the statement is false; a score of 10 demonstrates that a statement describes your needs perfectly.

1. I love what I do. …… out of 10.
2. My work stimulates me. …… out of 10.
3. My work inspires me. …… out of 10.
4. I find it easy to get out of bed in the mornings. …… out of 10.
5. The amount that I am paid meets my day-to-day requirements …… out of 10.
6. I feel appreciated and valued by my colleagues. …… out of 10.

If you have scored yourself below 7 for any of these, continue to the worksheet.

WORKSHEET

If you are about to fill out this worksheet, it is because your current job or career is not meeting all your needs. Your Career Threads could be stronger than they are. So what are you going to do about it? Situations don't improve by themselves: positive transformation requires positive action.

Consider every low-scoring statement carefully, then write down three actions that could improve your score, following the example printed below. Be realistic, and embark on your proposed courses of action as soon as you can.

Example

This is how the action plan could be filled out by someone who scored below 7 for 'The amount that I am paid meets my day-to-day requirements'.

	ACTION	DATE COMPLETED
1	Collect a 'dossier' of my positive work appraisals and praise from customers	
2	Go on the internet and research the best ways to ask for a pay rise	
3	Armed with my dossier and knowledge, arrange to meet my boss and ask for a pay rise	

Fill out this action plan if you scored below 7 for 'I love what I do'.

	ACTION	DATE COMPLETED
1		
2		
3		

Fill out this action plan if you scored below 7 for 'My work stimulates me'.

	ACTION	DATE COMPLETED
1		
2		
3		

Fill out this action plan if you scored below 7 for 'My work inspires me'.

	ACTION	DATE COMPLETED
1		
2		
3		

Fill out this action plan if you scored below 7 for 'I find it easy to get out of bed in the mornings'.

	ACTION	DATE COMPLETED
1		
2		
3		

Fill out this action plan if you scored below 7 for 'The amount that I am paid meets my day-to-day requirements'.

	ACTION	DATE COMPLETED
1		
2		
3		

Fill out this action plan if you scored below 7 for 'I feel appreciated and valued by my colleagues'.

	ACTION	DATE COMPLETED
1		
2		
3		

If these measures do not work, or if you have concluded that your current Career Threads are beyond repair, continue to the following chapter.

CHAPTER

The career guideposts

Good Career Threads don't appear out of thin air. As the rope maker, it is down to you to create them. Your current career may delight you; if this is the case, skip to the next chapter. But if you are stuck in a job that frustrates you because you feel that you could – and should – be doing better, read on.

The actions and worksheets below are slotted into three guideposts.

- **First guidepost**. You know that you want to move on, but you don't know where to begin or where to go.
- **Second guidepost**. You know where your untapped talents lie, but you don't know how to narrow them down or turn one into a new career.
- **Third guidepost**. You have a crystal-clear idea about what you want to do and where you want to be, and you are ready to compile a sound plan of action.

Once you have found 'the thing that makes your heart sing', you can transform your vision into a successful career, find fulfilment and weave professional achievements throughout your Golden Rope. Together, these guideposts create a roadmap that will take you there.

First guidepost: searching for inspiration

This worksheet will help you if:

- you seek a new career;
- you are unsure where your greatest talents lie;
- you don't know where to begin.

1. Make a list of up to five of your hobbies; pick out the ones that you enjoy most and consider if you would like to carve a career out of any of them. For example, if you enjoy visiting stately homes and sites of historic interest, would you be interested in a career in tourism, or conservation?

a. _____

b. _____

c. _____

d. _____

e. _____

2. Ask your family and friends where your strengths and talents lie. People who are close to you, who have observed you over many months or years, are well placed to highlight your good points. They may even surprise you with their opinions! Take the three comments or ideas that inspire and interest you most, and list them here.

a. _____

b. _____

c. _____

3. Look back on your schooldays, or read through your old school reports. In which subjects did you excel? Remember the subjects that captured your imagination. Once you have left education and set out upon a career path, it is easy to forget that you displayed strength in other fields too. List your strongest subjects here, and consider if you would like to carve a career out of any of them.

a. _____

b. _____

c. _____

4. Read through local business directories, freesheets or the jobs section of your favourite newspaper. Do any of the listed industries, occupations or roles interest you? If so, list the most appealing ones here. Don't dismiss anything that may appear, at first glance, to be beyond your talents or experiences. Open your vision!

a. _____

b. _____

c. _____

5. Even if you are stuck in a job or career that you dislike, are there any parts of your working day that you enjoy? For example, a sales executive may dislike face-to-face contact, but enjoy the admin or report-writing associated with the role. A taxi driver may be weary of driving around the same 'patch', but appreciate the independence of his or her working lifestyle. Many of us are inclined to focus upon what we do not like, but what we do like is more important. Draw out any positive features of your current role, and list them here.

a. _____

b. _____

c. _____

6. Look around you. Rake through your everyday life. Catch yourself saying, 'I'd love to do that'. If you work for a company, is there a department or a role to which you are drawn because it appears to be more attractive than your present position? If you are a full-time parent preparing to re-enter the working world outside the home, which part of your day do you find to be the most stimulating – and could this be the seed of a new career choice? List any ideas here.

a. _____

b. _____

c. _____

d. _____

e. _____

7. Once you have filled out this section, you will have a list of possible career ideas. Your next step is to boil these down to three responsibilities, roles or fields of expertise that – for whatever reason – appeal to you most.

a. _____

b. _____

c. _____

Now that you have three ideas in place, you can proceed to the second guidepost and begin exploring your chosen options. If none are 'runners' by the time you reach the end of this chapter, return to this section and choose others. If you have filled out every space above, you will have 22 career ideas. There is a good chance that at least one of them will be right for you.

Second guidepost: setting the pace
This worksheet will help you if:

- you seek a new career,
- you know where your talents lie,
- you know which fields or areas of work interest you; however, you haven't yet narrowed your choices, or formed a clear picture in your head of what it is that you want to do and where it is that you want to be.

1. Explore your motivations. For each good idea that you have for a new career, ask yourself *why*? If you are looking at a career in film, for example, *why* do you want this? Is it because you eat, sleep and breathe film? Is it because you want to work alongside actors? Is it because you would be stimulated and inspired by being around creative people? If you cannot come up with at least three answers to this question, are you truly passionate about this career idea? You may wish to reconsider your options.

First career idea: . . . .
Why? . . . .
Why? . . . .
Why? . . . .

Second career idea (if appropriate): . . . .
Why? . . . .
Why? . . . .
Why? . . . .

Third career idea (if appropriate): . . . .
Why? . . . .
Why? . . . .
Why? . . . .

2.   Visit the careers section of your local library, and research the industries and career paths that interest you. Aim to learn the following:

First career idea: . . . .

a.   Entry routes. How do you get 'into' it?
     . . . .
     . . . .
     . . . .

b.   Qualifications required.
     . . . .
     . . . .
     . . . .

c.   Various roles.
     . . . .
     . . . .
     . . . .
     . . . .
     . . . .

. . . .

d.   Pay scales.

. . . .

. . . .

. . . .

e.   Prospects.

. . . .

. . . .

. . . .

f.   Other advantages and disadvantages of each chosen field. Can you expect a pension? Will you have to work antisocial hours? Are there family-friendly working environments?

Advantages:. . . . .

. . . .

. . . .

Disadvantages:. . . . .

. . . .

. . . .

Second career idea (if appropriate):. . . . .

a.   Entry routes. How do you get 'into' it?

. . . .

. . . .

. . . .

b.   Qualifications required.

. . . .

. . . .

. . . .

c.   Various roles.

. . . .

. . . .

. . . .

. . . .

....

....

d. Pay scales.

....

....

....

e. Prospects.

....

....

....

f. Other advantages and disadvantages of each chosen field. Can you expect a pension? Will you have to work antisocial hours? Are there family-friendly working environments?

Advantages:..

....

....

Disadvantages:.......................................

....

....

Third career idea (if appropriate): ....

a. Entry routes. How do you get 'into' it?

....

....

....

b. Qualifications required.

....

....

....

c. Various roles.

....

....

. . . .
. . . .
. . . .
. . . .

d.   Pay scales.

. . . .
. . . .
. . . .

e.   Prospects.

. . . .
. . . .
. . . .

f.   Other advantages and disadvantages of each chosen field. Can
     you expect a pension? Will you have to work antisocial hours?
     Are there family-friendly working environments?
     Advantages:. . . . .
     . . . .
     . . . .
     Disadvantages:. . . . .
     . . . .
     . . . .

If you are unable to locate all of this information, ask a librarian to
assist you. Make notes of the answers, and read these notes back to
yourself when you get home. Are your chosen career options still
desirable to you? Discard any that aren't.

3. Learn more about yourself. Psychometric testing measures
abilities, attitudes and personality traits. Employers use it to select
team members who are best suited to their organisations' needs. If
you have not done so before, test yourself. Links to various free, online
tests can be found at www.yourgoldenthreads.com. The results will
help you to decide if you are suited to your chosen options.

Test conclusions: ....
....
....
....
....

4. Put part of your social life to one side, and put that saved time to good use. Strengthen your Learning Threads by securing employment experience within your chosen field. If you are considering a career in healthcare or medicine, for example, you could test the waters by becoming a hospital auxiliary or joining the St John Ambulance. If you want to own a restaurant, go and work in one. By gaining this work experience, you will upgrade your industry knowledge and boost your CV in all the right places. Furthermore, you will be able to make an informed decision as to whether your chosen career can live up to your expectations.

When you have completed all these actions, you are on the right path. To create a plan of action that will make your dream career a reality, proceed to the third guidepost.

Third guidepost: reaching your destination

This worksheet will help you if:

- you seek a new career;
- you know where your talents lie;
- you know which fields or areas of work interest you;
- you know what you want to do and where you want to be;
- you have yet to compile and follow an informed plan of action, to get to where you want to be.

1. Forge new Relationship Threads. Seek out and mix with people who work or have worked within your chosen field, and introduce yourself. The more senior, distinguished and experienced they are, the better. Ask them tough questions and, afterwards, make notes of their answers.

a. What is it like to be them?

....
....
....
....

b. What are the most challenging aspects of their day-to-day working life?

....
....
....
....

c. What are the highs and the lows?
Highs:...
....
Lows: ....
....

d. How did they get started?

....
....
....
....

e. What practical advice can they offer to someone starting out?

....
....
....
....

Take this information and use it to take informed steps towards your new career. Such meetings will also furnish you with valuable contacts who, in certain circumstances, could even provide you with your first big break.

2. Make best use of your Productivity Threads by mapping your goals. Draw up a detailed plan that includes time-frames, requirements and costs. Leading motivational coach and author Brian Mayne says: 'Goal setting is a natural function of the brain. Making a decision triggers a subconscious process that transforms the decision into a deed.' He has developed an extremely successful Goal Mapping programme, which he describes as the 'master skill for achievement in all areas of life'. Visit his website, www.goalmapping. com, to download free instructions and Goal Mapping templates.

3. Draw strength from your Family Threads. Your family may be able to keep you motivated during difficult times. You will also benefit from their confidence and support, especially if your career ambitions require the family to move, administer temporary cutbacks or make other sacrifices.

4. Above all, keep going! What all successful people have in common is that they never gave up. They didn't surrender their ambitions during difficult times; instead, they pressed on despite rejections, complications and other setbacks. Be like them. Take those knocks and blows, but stay upright and keep moving towards your ambitions.

Every time you take a step closer to your career goal – even if it is a baby step, such as meeting a new contact or receiving a relevant compliment from a friend, family member or colleague – make a note of it here . By filling out this progress table, you can build and maintain your momentum.

DATE	DETAILS OF PROGRESS
01/02/09	Requested details and brochures, via phone and e-mail, of the five top courses

If you think your best thoughts, make your best plans and take your best actions, your life will move in one direction: upwards. Right now, the career that you seek and deserve could be a speck in the distance. But keep pushing on, and your future will spread out and grow before your eyes.

Make the most of your Career Threads. Sit tight, and enjoy the ride.

CHAPTER 6

The career
casebook

T he following case studies show how Career Threads can be formed and developed, regardless of age, schooling, background or circumstances. You don't have to be a genius or a superstar to enjoy a successful and rewarding career, marking achievements that enhance all areas of your life.

Case study 1: Gerald

Gerald Burton had been the manager of a paint shop, but he found the work to be uninspiring and stressful. He came from a working-class background and had entered employment with the sole ambition of improving upon what his parents had achieved. He then took a job as a salesman for an insurance company, but received little support from his managers and did not enjoy the work. He became so frustrated and miserable that he began to experience regular panic attacks on his way to work in the mornings.

After he decided that it was time to make changes in his life, Gerald signed up for a three-day course on effective business presentation.

The course transformed his life.

At the end of the first session, Gerald watched a video playback of a mock presentation that he had given, seeing himself as others saw him for the first time. He saw that even though he had been extremely nervous during filming, it didn't show. Instead, he came across as confident and knowledgeable. Other people on the course were very positive about his efforts; they told him he was a 'natural' speaker, who had clearly been enjoying himself up there. Little did they know that he had been dreading his turn to speak. Gerald had discovered his untapped talents. He decided that he wouldn't stay any longer than he had to in his sales job. He began to build his Career Threads

At school he had been a keen mathematician, and among his friends he was known for his knack with numbers. So, at evenings and weekends, Gerald trained to become a financial adviser. After he qualified, he resigned and went on to found his own financial advice business, making investment-themed presentations to large groups. His in-depth knowledge of his subject, combined with his charm and his ability to get results for his customers, led to numerous word-of-mouth recommendations. Gerald's reputation spread and his success grew.

As Gerald's Career Threads became strong, he also worked on his Learning Threads, gaining additional qualifications. He went from selling personal insurance products to making big money investments on behalf of companies and wealthy individuals. Aged 50, he was able to scale down his work commitments while maintaining a high level of income, so that he could take frequent holidays and spend more time with his four grandchildren.

He says: 'I'm not "Mr Average" anymore. Instead, I feel that my quality of life has doubled. I am earning twice the amount of money, I am living in a home that is twice as big and I take twice the number of holidays. My life today definitely has a buzz to it.'

Would you take a three-day course that could transform your life? How are you going to find such a course? How are you going to ensure that you extract maximum value from it?

 Food is one of my greatest passions. I believe that life is for living – and for me, good food adds a lot of pleasure to life. My wife, Janet, feels the same: she is a qualified chef, and makes the most delicious dishes you have ever tasted. They are so good that about ten years ago she began making products for friends and family on demand.

We knew a wholesale butcher, John Worsley, and invited him and his wife to go into business with us. They said yes. Within three days I had found a building in the nearby village, and we began fitting it out with commercial equipment. We didn't have any experience in the food industry and we didn't have any contacts, so we had taken on a lot of risk. But our enthusiasm for the product drove us forward.

Seven years on, our company has a multimillion pound turnover. We now supply our frozen products to all the UK's national supermarket chains. Right now Janet is overseeing and developing new recipes, while I am developing a new marketing campaign.

We both love what we do, no question about it. When we co-founded the company, I was an agent selling to car dealerships around the region. I do enjoy that work, but it doesn't engage and motivate me in the same way that food does. Janet had been a full-time mum, raising our three children, but they had grown up and she was in a position to channel her energies elsewhere. Our eldest son, Andrew, also works in our family business and has played a vital role in its development. Our daughter Emma, who works in recruitment, has helped us to find staff. Our youngest son, James, came to work at the factory during his university holidays. Our strong Family Threads and strong Career Threads are intertwined.

Other Golden Threads in our ropes have also helped us to climb towards success. In the Relationship Threads section of this book, I describe how our involvement with a group of food producers led us to our MD, Dennis. And we couldn't have achieved so much in such a short space of time if our Productivity Threads hadn't been so robust. We have also drawn upon our Learning Threads; for example, we had to take on a tremendous amount of research so that we could get the company up and running.

If you want to change your career, get creative. Spend your spare time mulling over ideas and giving your goals the time and attention that they deserve. Get the ball rolling and you'll be on your way. I have learned that passion and ambition create energy all on their own. When you get enough momentum behind you, you are able to knock down any obstacle that appears in your path.

Are you always on the lookout for new ideas and opportunities? When inspiration strikes, will you use all the energy and courage that you can muster to act upon it?

Case study 2: Margaret

Margaret Wood is the founder and MD of ICW UK Ltd, which produces high-strength glazing products to order. The company has clients around the world, and its glass been supplied to high-profile enterprises including Kew Gardens and Formula One. In 2002, she won a Women Inventors in Industry Award after developing a touch-sensitive window system for use on buses and trains. High-profile visitors to her Wakefield factory have included the Prime Minister, Gordon Brown, who has lauded her as a role model for businesswomen.

Her professional achievements demonstrate that when you are building a strong Golden Rope and you have found the thing that makes your heart sing, you can transform the most unlikely vision into reality. When she started out, Margaret had no engineering experience. Her Career Threads were formed out of raw pluck and determination.

Margaret left school aged 16, because her parents 'didn't consider it appropriate' for a young woman to attend university. She married at 20 and became a full-time housewife and mother. Her husband, Tony, owned his own business making industrial control panels.

When her three children were teenagers, Tony died aged just 47. Margaret was left with a family to support and no visible means of income. Her family and friends expected that she would marry again – one relative even told her that to continue as a single mother would be 'socially unacceptable'.

Struggling to come to terms with her loss and with her new life, Margaret had other ideas. Before he became ill, her husband had been working on a new idea for high-strength glazing for crane cabs. Moreover, he had always told her that she could achieve whatever she set her mind to. In 1993, Margaret decided to found ICW as a memorial to him. Despite her lack of business experience, she was determined to continue his work. She strengthened her Learning Threads 'on the job', wearing overalls and even driving the company's delivery van. Slowly, her expertise and her company's reputation grew.

Margaret says: 'There were times when I thought I had taken on too much, but I learned to look towards the future. My husband always believed in my abilities – but even so, I think he would be surprised and delighted by the company I have built up.'

When she started out, Margaret was quick to build Relationship Threads, getting to know local business leaders and becoming involved with a local trade-development agency. Now she is helping other women in her region to become involved in business life; she sits on the board of the networking and business support group Forward Ladies.

Every week without fail, the successful MD snaps on her rubber gloves and cleans her factory toilets.

'I've come a long way', she explains, 'and sometimes, when I look at who I used to be and who I am now, I can barely recognise myself. I don't want to forget my roots.

'Life takes away as much as it gives – but I believe that for the resilient amongst us, life's opportunities are there for the taking.'

If you want a dream career, how will you turn that career into your reality? Are you so passionate about it that you could flatten any barriers in your path? Are you prepared to hit the ground running?

My strongest Career Threads have grown out of my passion for creating something out of nothing. I founded a telecommunications company in 2000. By the time I sold it five years later, it had a multi-million turnover.

It wasn't my first shot at building a business in telecommunications; I was involved with another entrepreneur in 1995. This first effort was a financial disaster, but gave my Learning Threads a great boost. I learned to trust myself and my own judgement. I also learned that a partnership such as that one didn't suit me, because differing aims and priorities would lead a company sideways rather than forwards. I learned to pay myself before I paid banks and suppliers, and I bought into many important principles and techniques for money management.

I retained many of the staff from the first company when I founded the second, including a brilliant young employee called Andrew who became my business partner. That was nine years ago, and we are currently pursuing new ventures together. He was able to take charge of the company's day-to-day operations – a responsibility for which I had little appetite. His input meant that I could make the best possible use of my time. I could concentrate on what I did best and enjoyed most: growing the company and working on the business, rather than in it.

Our company managed fleets of mobile phones on behalf of corporate customers and government agencies. We oversaw upgrades and car phone installations for customers' employees. We also monitored employees' use of mobiles, identifying instances of abuse such as employees' personal calls, and use of work phones at weekends.

My Career Threads have drawn upon my strong Family Threads. My father-in-law and brother-in-law came and assisted with the finance department. My wife Jo worked in the debt collection department for two years. There was a sense that we were all in it together, and that only added to our shared determination to make a success of the enterprise.

66 A good, strong Career Thread doesn't have to be sleek and shiny from the outset. **99**

In my experience, a few knots, hooks and loops are fine. This goes for Learning Threads too. By the time we broke up the first company, I had learned my lessons the hard way. What I had learned came to serve me well for future enterprises.

If your career path is rockier than you had expected, how will you respond to its challenges? Will you give up and return to your old life, or will your determination to succeed carry you onwards?

Understand your values

Gerald and Margaret established new values for themselves when they changed their career directions. Are you clear about your own work and career values? These are your guideposts, showing you the way.

Are you able to answer the questions at the end of each case study? If you cannot, it may help if you sit down with somebody and they ask you these questions in an informal interview setting. Your answers will help you to evaluate your own career values and crystallise your future plans.

PART 3

The Wealth
Threads

CHAPTER

7

The well-to-do wallet

The following chapters are dedicated to improving your financial situation. Before you begin reading, there are two things that you should know.

The first is that this section isn't a 'get rich quick' guide. That quackery is best left to other books or Ponzi schemes. What is more, it is worth bearing in mind that money swiftly gained is often swiftly lost. The newspapers are littered with tales of lottery winners who have blown their fortunes.

The second point is that your Wealth Threads are closely knitted to your Spiritual Threads. Wealth, in its naked form, is defined in the dictionary as 'abundance of money or of precious commodities'. To a certain extent, however, your Wealth Threads are also an extension of your state of mind. One person's rainy day fund can be another person's sumptuous riches. Your personal definition of wealth is dictated by your background, your ambitions and your priorities in life. Rich is a feeling, not an amount of money.

It is part of human nature to want to be more, do more and have more. These desires push you towards a more abundant life. You cannot choose your starting point, but it is your vision, your plan and your actions that will create your Wealth Threads, one by one.

Why Wealth Threads are important

If you have financial security, you have strong Wealth Threads that bolster your Golden Rope, ease your climb and smooth your progress in life.

This is because Wealth Threads enrich other Golden Threads in your life: your Learning Threads and your Career Threads in particular. Money doesn't buy love or happiness, but it has its uses. It offers you a greater number of choices and ensures that you can make the most of opportunities. For example, if you are able to fund a training course that puts you within reach of your dream career, your Wealth Threads strengthen your Learning Threads, and your Learning Threads strengthen your Career Threads. In turn, your Career Threads strengthen your Wealth Threads. It's a positive chain reaction.

Wealth Threads nourish Spiritual Threads, because financial security improves peace of mind and enables you to live in comfort and style, organising your days with much greater ease. If wealth is a state of mind, it is also a very pleasant way of life.

Barriers to wealth

Wealth is there to work for you; it isn't there for you to spend willy-nilly. If debt worms its way into your day-to-day existence, to the point where it begins to go unnoticed, you will never become wealthy. Don't let it secure a foothold in your life.

o **Store cards**, which have sky-high interest rates, should be avoided like the plague if you are not always able to pay them off at the end of every month.

o **Credit cards** are tempting, but if you have to spend years repaying them, your journey to financial security will be prolonged. When offers pour through the letterbox, put them in your 'general file': the bin.

o **Avoid loans**, particularly those that are added to your outstanding mortgage. They will end up costing you a dispro-portionate amount in interest charges. They will also undermine your financial foundations.

Although this goes against conventional wisdom, windfalls can also be a barrier to wealth creation. If you haven't earned your money, you can be left rudderless when it lands in your bank account. For this reason, many lottery, pools and scratchcard winners have ended up no better off than they were before their wins. In the 1960s, pools winner Viv Nicholson became famous for her cry of 'Spend, spend, spend', but found her new riches difficult to manage and was declared bankrupt within 15 years. Former binman Michael Carroll won £9.7 million on the National Lottery in 2002; he promptly earned the nickname 'Lotto Lout' and is reported to have squandered much of his fortune upon a frenetic, drug-fuelled lifestyle.

However, when you work to strengthen your Wealth Threads over time, following a clear vision and earning financial security piece by piece, you will learn to manage your wealth along the way. When you are acutely conscious of your money's value, you are determined to spend and invest it wisely.

 Take charge. Don't be a prisoner of hope.

When I hit that all–time low, I was saddled with £35,000 of debts and had nothing to show for them. This was a stressful time, made worse by my knowledge that much of that money had been frittered on my old lifestyle. I knew that paying off those debts would be a long, painful process, but I couldn't have them hanging over my head if I was to move on and make a success of my life.

I began with a small, blank book. I wrote down all my liabilities and also began entering every financial transaction. This meant that I could assess how much I owed, and how much I was spending.

Next, I drew up a detailed plan to get myself back into the black. I worked out that, as driven as I was, my income at the time meant that it would take me six years to pay off all the debt. I engaged an accountant, who successfully negotiated lower payment rates with my creditors, and I paid the sums off piecemeal.

Making that final payment, I felt wonderful. I was back to the black: no debt, no one chasing me, no worries and far less pressure. I could turn all of my attention to the creation of wealth and the strengthening of my Wealth Threads.

This experience left me with a strong sense of financial discipline. It has also left me rather risk-adverse; I have worked so hard for my wealth that I am unwilling to gamble it. With the markets in turmoil, I can't say that I regret this strategy.

I should add that Family Threads have played a key role in the strengthening of my Wealth Threads. My wife Jo has always saved as much money as possible. Thanks to her efforts, once I was debt-free we were able to fund the set-up costs for my first telecommunications company. Even now, we save more than 40 per cent of our net income. Our financial discipline continues to pay dividends – in more ways than one.

Eight strides to stronger Wealth Threads

1. Take charge. Don't count on winning the National Lottery, Premium Bonds or inheriting from long-lost relatives. Don't be a prisoner to hope. It is almost certainly true that the only person who will generate your wealth is you. So what are you going to do about it? When? And how?

2. Strengthen your Health Threads. Do whatever it takes to make them as strong as they can be, because if you feel terrible, life often looks terrible. If you feel incredibly well, you can do incredible things.

3. Start your own business. Even if you don't have any money to invest, you do not see yourself as a natural entrepreneur or you are content in your career, find a way to generate a second income. This could be a full-time initiative or a franchise opportunity, or an online affiliate programme.

One of the best examples of an affiliation programme belongs to the UK telecommunications company Daisy Group (www.daisyaffiliate.com). For as little as £3 per week, Daisy affiliates can create a secondary revenue for your business equal to that of a salary.

What happens next is down to you. Your business could take off and become a successful career; your eBay activities could provide a little extra pin money to invest or spend as you please. The principle remains the same: to become wealthy you must take control of your income, whatever the amount, and take steps towards financial independence. Become a self-starter, or edge towards self-sufficiency and you will boost your talents for gathering wealth.

 Financial self-sufficiency is critical to self-worth.

4. Never make large purchases on a whim. Give yourself plenty of time to mull over an expensive purchase before taking action. It stands to reason that if you spend unwisely, or if you are regularly afflicted with buyer's remorse, you will find it difficult to accumulate wealth.

5. Monitor your expenditure closely. Develop a strong sense of discipline, and stay in control of your finances – don't let them control you. When your bank statement lands on the doormat, don't shove it into a drawer. Take the time to go through it, checking off every item against your receipts and records. Create a house file for your finances. If your gas and electricity bills go up, offset that rise by finding a cheaper provider or slashing your budget elsewhere. Keep your expenditure on an even keel.

6. Never borrow for a depreciating asset. If you borrow money to pay for expensive goods such as cars or entertainment systems, your finances are taking a double whack. You are forking out interest charges on loans or credit cards; all the while, the cash value of those products is swiftly deteriorating. Save up for expensive goods; whenever possible, fund these purchases with money that you already have. When you pay in cash, you can get the best deals.

I had a spell working in car sales. I vividly remember a young couple coming into our showroom, to pay for their first car with cash that they had saved. I was impressed. Before they drove away, the man asked me how much it would have cost them every month if they had purchased the car with a loan. I did the sums and told him the amount, which was in the region of £250 per month.

A couple of years later, the couple returned to buy a beautiful Volvo. They traded in their first car, and paid cash on the outstanding balance. It turned out that every month since buying that first car, they had stashed £250 per month into a savings account. Then they had withdrawn the total amount in full, to pay the balance needed for their second car. The short-term pain of saving for that first vehicle led to long-term gain. What a brilliant, simple idea! If you used this system for all your major purchases, how much easier would your life be?

7. Chart your net worth. At the end of every month, deduct your total assets from your total liabilities and produce a table or graph that shows your overall net worth. Assets include homes, cars, savings, stocks, valuables and pensions. Liabilities include mortgage balances, credit card debts, overdrafts and loans. If you go to www.networthiq.com, you can create a graph showing how your net worth is improving (or otherwise!) over time. This will help you to monitor your finances and – once your monthly chart shows that your net worth is rising – supply you with additional motivation to keep up the good work.

8. Draw upon your Relationship Threads. Seek out financial mentors: successful people whose wealth management has attracted your admiration. Ask them how they got to where they are, and extract as much advice from them as you can.

I befriended an extremely successful businessman at just the right time. His name was Peter Morris. He had started out as a small-time carpenter, travelling to jobs with planks of wood strapped to the handlebars of his bicycle. By the time I met him, he had built a multimillion pound kitchen business and was driving a Rolls-Royce. He became a member of my first health club in the mid-1970s. After I became friendly with him and discovered his career history, I asked him for advice on my company's finances. At this time the club had been open for more than three years; our bank manager was monitoring its progress closely, and I felt that there was much room for improvement in my management of financial matters. So did the bank manager! Peter said that he would tell me what to do, on the condition that I went away and acted on his advice. I agreed to do so. He told me that when he was growing up his family was poor and his mother had always divided what little money the family had into small boxes for rent, gas and food shopping. The boxes were kept on the mantelpiece, and none of her children ever dared touch them. Although Peter had become a wealthy businessman, this habit stayed with him and he ran all of his companies using a similar method. This unyielding discipline was, he told me, the backbone of his financial success.

After Peter explained this, he instructed me to open several business bank accounts: one for each of my health club's overheads. He told me to set up direct debits, and to arrange for monies to be automatically transferred from my main business bank account to the overhead accounts on a weekly basis. What was left in the main business bank account represented the club's profits.

I found that this idea was as effective as it was straightforward. It didn't cost anything, and at a glance I could see how well the club was faring. Before I knew it, our main account held more than £3,000 in profits – no mean feat, in the 1970s.

Be ready for bumps

 Expect the best. Prepare for the worst.

Even when you are gathering wealth and everything is going well, you can never tell what lies around the corner.

In September 2008, the world's economies experienced meltdown. Banks and individuals were suddenly left exposed. In 2007, 26,200 homes were repossessed in the UK; in 2009 the Council of Mortgage Lenders was estimating that 65,000 homes would be repossessed. In 2007, 40 small businesses were closing every week in the UK; in 2009, this figure rose to 120 closures a day. Events such as these go to show that, no matter how rosy appearances may be, outside forces can wield unexpected new challenges.

An ability to adapt to new circumstances will serve you well. Accept that your Wealth Threads will not wind smoothly; there will be bumps along the way. If your Threads are resilient, however, they will regain their gleam. You can prepare for the unexpected with three pre-emptive steps:

1. If you have a **credit card**, get into the habit of using it as a purchasing tool, rather than as a rich seam of ready funds. Only use it for purchases that you can and will clear in full at the end of every month. If you are currently in debt to credit card companies, make it a priority to pay off those cards as soon as possible. If you fear that you are in above your head, seek assistance sooner rather than later. The National Debtline (www.nationaldebtline.co.uk / 0808 808 4000) provides free, confidential advice and support.

2. Keep a **rainy day fund** in a savings account. Ideally, it should contain enough money to support your household for several months. Save at least 10 per cent of your income every month, not to be touched under any circumstances, and you will raise this amount relatively quickly.

3. Stay a step ahead, by drawing up a **contingency plan** that outlines your planned course of action, should any catastrophe occur. It's a 'What if' list: what would happen if you lost your best customer? What would happen if your car broke down tomorrow? Paint the list of worst-case scenarios as black as you can. Consider the list carefully, and come up with answers and solutions.

SUMMARY

○ Wealth Threads bolster your Golden Rope by providing financial security that eases your climb and smoothes your progress in life.

○ Wealth Threads are an extension of your state of mind. Your definition of wealth is dictated by your background, your ambitions and your priorities.

○ If debt worms its way into your day-to-day existence, you will never become wealthy. If it has secured a foothold in your life, it will spread like a disease.

○ Draw upon your other Golden Threads and edge towards self-sufficiency, and you will take important steps towards wealth creation.

○ Expect the best, but prepare for the worst. Even when everything is going well, you cannot know what lies around the corner.

ACTION POINTS

1. Get into good habits now, and they will serve you well as your wealth accumulates. If you stuff your bills and bank statements into a drawer, now is the time to put them in order. Juggle bills and they will take over your life; know what is coming out of your bank account and when, and you can turn your attention elsewhere.

2. Wealth is a state of mind. So close your eyes, sit back and imagine: for you, what does being wealthy look like? How does it feel? Different people have different ideas. For one person, it may be paying off the mortgage on the family home; for another, it may be moving into a large mansion and having staff to attend to every waking need. Whatever your vision is, once you have identified it you can begin to move towards it.

3. How much money will you need to turn your vision into reality? How long will it take? What are the variables? What changes do you need to make? How, with further effort, can this book help you to achieve this? Sit down with pen and paper, work out your answers and draw up your plan. If you went to Brian Maynes website (www.goalmapping.com) and created a Goal Map after reading the Career Threads section, why not revisit that website and create a new Goal Map for your Wealth Threads?

W O R K S H E E T

This worksheet brings together a number of small but significant foundation steps to gathering wealth. It is suitable for everyone, from low earners to high earners, and asks you to seek out and take note of the best deals for your monthly overheads.

The aim of this worksheet is to streamline your day-to-day expenditure. The less you spend, the less likely you are to find that there is too much month at the end of your money. When your income exceeds your outgoings, you are in the best possible position to create strong Wealth Threads.

You will need:

- your bank statements;
- your bank card details;
- your recent household bills;
- an internet connection (This will enable you to visit price comparison sites such as www.moneysupermarket.com and www.uswitch.com, to find the best money-saving deals on many of the overheads listed below).

Examples

MORTGAGE

Best available deal

Current mortgage deal expires 12.10. I meet criteria for 3-year fixed rate deal with another bank whose contact details are:

Tel — 020 7000 0000 Email — mortgages@thebank.com

Current cost per month	New cost per month	Money saved
£830	£809	£21

GAS

Best available deal

Cheapest provider is Gas Unltd and can change via their website or through a price comparison site

Current cost per month	New cost per month	Money saved
£49	£41	£8

MORTGAGE/RENT

Best available deal

Current cost per month	New cost per month	Money saved

GAS

Best available deal

Current cost per month	New cost per month	Money saved

ELECTRICITY

Best available deal

Current cost per month	New cost per month	Money saved

TELEPHONE/INTERNET/TV

Best available deal

Current cost per month	New cost per month	Money saved

MOBILE PHONE

Best available deal

Current cost per month	New cost per month	Money saved

CONTENTS INSURANCE

Best available deal

Current cost per month	New cost per month	Money saved

LIFE INSURANCE

Best available deal

Current cost per month	New cost per month	Money saved

CAR INSURANCE

Best available deal

Current cost per month	New cost per month	Money saved

LOANS

Best available deal

Current cost per month	New cost per month	Money saved

CREDIT CARDS

Best available deal

Current cost per month	New cost per month	Money saved

OTHER:

Best available deal

Current cost per month	New cost per month	Money saved

OTHER:

Best available deal

Current cost per month	New cost per month	Money saved

It's notable, isn't it, how small savings here and there can together add up to a significant sum every month? You may find that selected overheads, such as subscriptions to magazines that you rarely read, or memberships that you use infrequently, can be eliminated altogether. The next chapter will show you how to manage your surplus income effectively.

CHAPTER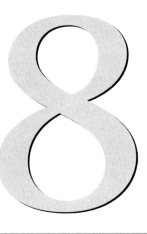

Hold on to your wallet

Look around your local bookshop, or on www.amazon.co.uk, and you'll find no end of bestsellers telling you how to become rich beyond your wildest dreams. These books sell well, because they appeal to a wide range of people. After all, who doesn't want financial freedom?

There are relatively few books that show you how to safeguard your wealth once you have created it. Perhaps this is because the target market is smaller, and the subject less glamorous. Perhaps there is an unwritten assumption that if you know how to make money, you will know how to look after it. In real life, this isn't always the case. As many rags-to-riches-to-rags stories have shown, people who become wealthy don't necessarily stay wealthy.

Wealth Threads can be the most fragile of all the threads in your Golden Rope. If they are not kept in tip-top condition they will swiftly fade, fray or, even worse, snap.

This chapter is a mini-guide to keeping your Wealth Threads strong. It is tailored to those who have already achieved a good level of financial security. That said, don't skip it if you are still working towards this security.

 The best habits are those learned early.

Dips and troughs

Here are some of the most common reasons why Wealth Threads slide through people's hands.

- **Their bank accounts expand – but so does their expenditure**. They build an enviable new lifestyle with their wealth, but lack of financial discipline means that, inevitably, they lose control of their spending. This is especially true of those who 'come into money' unexpectedly, without earning the right to it. Easy come, easy go.

- **They begin to believe their own PR**. So pleased are they with their financial conquests, they become convinced that they now know everything. For some, Learning Threads become dull and worn, and decision-making skills become tarnished. Others allow their drive and their work ethic to disintegrate.

- **They live for the present**, with an eye on their short-term future, but fail to plan adequately for the long term. For example, they may become preoccupied with spending money rather than making it, or they do not bother to build a decent pension or secure investment portfolio. They may leave their nest egg languishing in a bank account, slowly eroding in value over the years because the bank's interest rate cannot keep pace with inflation. Or they take daring risks, but find themselves overtaken by unexpected events.

When I lost my home, my chain of health clubs and my high net worth in 1990, I learned a difficult but valuable lesson.

My wealth disappeared very suddenly. It was as if my 25 years of hard work and achievements were deleted overnight. My problems began when I borrowed money from the bank and took a 10,000-square-foot space in a new shopping centre, to begin realising my vision of a state-of-the-art fitness centre. We were going to have an aerobics dance floor, and a mezzanine level that gave us half as much space again. Our architects' designs were stunning.

Problems arose when the shopping centre's multiplex cinema took out a court injunction against us, because the noise from the building work was interrupting their showings. After that we had to build the club at night, which turned out to be twice as expensive. At around the same time, bank interest rates soared from 8 per cent to 15 per cent. Combined, these factors increased our building costs by £150,000. We were unable to cover that amount, but it was too late to turn back. A former employee contacted one of the club's key suppliers to tell them that the company's finances were in trouble – and everything came crashing down.

Thankfully, this sad tale has a happy ending. My firm grip upon the Golden Threads in my life meant that I was able to haul myself back up again. I cannot deny, however, that it was a challenge.

If I could turn back time, I would not allow myself to become mired in such a vulnerable situation. I learned not to rely on banks: they had put us on an 'umbrella programme', which provided various lines of credit. But as soon as the rain came, they took that umbrella away. They didn't offer any advice or support, even though I had been a profitable customer for more than 15 years. I learned never to load all my success on to a single roll of the dice. I learned that if your spending increases when you are halfway through a project, make sure that your figures are still sound and adapt your financial plan accordingly. I learned never to overexpose myself in this way again.

Six ways to safeguard your finances

1.　Keep your wallet or purse tidy. A busy, messy wallet indicates that its owner is not in control of his or her finances. Ideally, you should know the value of the cash inside your wallet to the nearest £10, at all times. Arrange your banknotes neatly, and order them by value. Not only can you see how much money you have at a glance, but it is a frequent reminder that you control your finances – not the other way round. Any items that you do not need or use regularly can be discarded, or kept in a safe place. If you have three bank accounts but use only one, why carry three cards? Keep two at home; if you do not do this and your wallet is stolen or lost, you will have to cancel three times the number of cards.

2. Keep your wits about you and trust your instincts. If an idea, scheme or offer looks too good to be true, it probably is.

3. Know how compound interest works. This makes your money grow at a faster rate and plays an important role in your personal economics, yet some people are still fuzzy about how it works. When your money is growing in a savings account with an interest rate, you don't just earn interest on your original deposit. You also earn interest on the interest earned on that deposit. The longer you save for, the more your savings snowball. Over time, compound interest makes more money than simple interest, which is restricted to the original deposit. Note that when compound interest is applied to debts, they grow faster too.

4. Keep records that can be easily accessed. 'Lost and stolen' telephone numbers for bankcards are usually printed on the cards themselves – well thought through, eh? If you are comfortable with the security issues – and it should be stressed that if you are not, you should not do this – copy details of your bankcards to your Hotmail, Googlemail or Yahoo account. Give the message a nondescript subject title. Then, if your wallet is lost or stolen, you can access these details wherever you are in the world and cancel your cards with minimal fuss.

5. Don't keep your eggs in one basket. Calamitous events on the world financial markets in 2008 demonstrated the dangers of storing wealth in one place. When banks failed, savers lost money. Pension portfolios nose-dived. Your wealth is safest when it is spread out.

6. If you are self-employed, find an accountant. Even if you are capable of filling out your own tax return, consider outsourcing this chore. A good accountant can offer you sound financial advice, find the most tax-efficient ways to manage your income and create savings that exceed his or her fee.

I used to keep my wealth in two bank accounts. Now I have distributed it among eight of them. In view of subsequent events on the world's markets in 2008, I am pleased that I acted when I did.

I also benefit from the services of a first-class accountant. In 2007 his firm saved me more than £240,000 in one transaction and then a further £34,000 in 2008. The fees came to less than £2,500.

SUMMARY

o   Becoming wealthy and staying wealthy are two disciplines, not one. Once you have created strong Wealth Threads, you must strive to keep them in good condition.

o   You can – and should – take a number of simple measures to ensure that your financial security is not plunged into peril.

CHAPTER 9

ut your wallet
to work

Compound interest isn't limited to your bank account. It applies to your Wealth Threads too. You worked for your money – so why not make your money work for you?

This chapter focuses upon how your regular savings can be put to best use. The initial amounts that you save may be small but, compounded over time, they will begin to grow.

66 An income shouldn't be a means to an end; it should be a means to a beginning. 99

Think of it this way. Were you to spend time and money recruiting and paying a member of staff – a cleaner, say, or a builder – would you permit them to sit around doing nothing? Probably not. So why should your relationship with your money be any different? It is there to serve you, so why leave it standing idle?

Here is an example – an extraordinary one, admittedly – of what can be achieved. Paul Navone is a retired American factory worker in his late seventies. He left school without any qualifications, worked for more than 62 years and never made more than £6.75 an hour. Today he is a multimillionaire.

Paul Navone has been able to amass his fortune because he has always lived simply and invested wisely. He doesn't own a television and he drives an old car. He ploughed his wages into savings and the stock market, finding four stockbrokers he could trust and investing in 'a little bit of everything' with a view to long-term gain. In 2008 he donated more than £1 million to colleges in his New Jersey neighbourhood.

Risky business

Different investment options suit different people and carry varying degrees of risk, which can be summarised as follows:

- **Low risk**: Premium Bonds, government bonds, treasury deposit schemes, high interest bank accounts and reinvestment in your own business.

- **Medium risk**: Investment in the FTSE 100: the large companies that are household names.

- **High risk**: Investment in someone else's big idea, other stocks, emerging technologies or countries.

When the potential returns are high, the risks are often high as well. The general rule of thumb is that *you should never risk more than you are prepared to lose.*

Pursue adventurous opportunities by all means, but only if you would be able to withstand the loss of your capital.

When you put your wealth to work, the choices that you make will be heavily influenced by your situation and experiences. If you are 23 and single, your investment portfolio could be more courageous than that of a 49-year-old who has a young family to support.

You should also draw upon your specialist experience and knowledge whenever possible. When you are able to explore investment opportunities within your field of employment, be it medicine, telecommunications or industrial cleaning, you are better placed to make informed investment decisions.

At the same time, don't let your background become a barrier to successful investments elsewhere. Draw upon other threads in your Golden Rope: when your Learning and Spiritual Threads are strong, you will have the energy and confidence to broaden your horizons at will. Look at Sheena Easton: the Scottish pop singer's showbiz career dipped, but she went on to gather an estimated £40 million fortune from shrewd property investments in Florida.

Six ways to send your money out to work

1. Banks and building societies. Turmoil on the markets has left a number of financial institutions flailing but, overall, banks and building societies are considered to be safe houses for your money. The downside: their ranges of high interest bonds and savings accounts may seem attractive at first sight, but will never make your money work to its full potential.

After selling our telecommunications company, Jo and I deposited the money in a Guaranteed Investment Plan while we decided what to do. The GIP's term was fixed for a year, the interest rate was 6.36 per cent and 90 per cent of our capital was guaranteed. We were content to leave our cash there; it earned part-time money until we found full-time work for it.

2. Government-backed investments. These are safe havens but, like banks, will not produce the highest returns. Examples of investment opportunities include treasury deposit schemes and index-linked government securities, known as 'linkers', which are linked to inflation. (Be aware, however, that when deflation occurs your money will be laid low for a while.) Money invested in Premium Bonds does not earn interest and the chances of winning are slight; however, capital is protected, which is something to bear in mind. In today's uncertain climate, investing in Premium Bonds is preferable to stashing your cash under your bed.

3. The stock market. There are many ways to play on the stock market. Investment opportunities include unit trusts, bonds, stock-brokers, day trades and unit-linked pension funds.

If this avenue interests you, proceed with caution: there are more sharks swimming in the stock exchanges than there are off the coast of Queensland. If you intend to invest significant amounts, it is advisable to first polish your Learning Threads until they dazzle.

I belong to the Wealth Enhancement Forum: a learning and development membership organisation for high net worth individuals. I joined so that I could learn more about sending my wealth out to work. It has been a valuable decision. I am now surrounded by others who are in a similar position to mine; together we learn and explore opportunities. We worked hard for our wealth, so why would we risk it without knowing what we were getting ourselves into?

4. Property. Until recently, property was regarded as a foolproof cash cow. Even now, reports of the buy-to-let market's demise have been exaggerated: if you have the money to buy, the best time to buy is when the markets are depressed. In time, the return on your investment will accumulate.

However, make it a rule of thumb to refrain from investing in residential or commercial property until you know current market conditions inside out. It used to be that you could buy a second property, sit back as property values soared, then sell your investment on for a handsome gain. This is no longer the case.

If you live in your property investment and house prices rise by 30 per cent, how much have you gained, really? After all, the next house that you buy will also be 30 per cent more expensive. One school of thought argues that you cannot draw long-term profits from property unless you buy into it when prices are thudding along the bottom. This is because a property doesn't grow by itself. It gobbles running costs: utilities, rates, maintenance charges and more.

There are some landlords who have generated enormous wealth from bricks and mortar, but bear in mind that when you purchase a property you are purchasing work, not a passive stream of income. Resources will have to be devoted to it on an ongoing basis.

Even when you are keen to buy at the bottom, it is difficult to tell when that bottom has been reached. Few of us are blessed with foresight, so it is likely that you will have to make an educated guess. If property values drop further following your purchase, returns will be longer in coming. So be it.

You can, however, boost your chances of securing a bargain by avoiding local estate agents in favour of building societies, local receivers and accountants. Leave your card and explain what you want to do. Encourage them to contact you with information about any potential opportunities, now or in the future. In the meantime, make a list of addresses for sale in your desired location, and review your list on a monthly basis. When a property has been on the market for a prolonged period, try knocking on the door and offering a bargain price.

5. If you choose to invest in property, stick to **nearby locations** if you can. Many overseas development schemes are high-risk investment opportunities. Bulgaria, for example, is frequently named as a property 'hotspot' – but oversupply has become an issue and tens of thousands of its newly built investment properties lie empty.

6. Shares in a start-up. This is high risk, because more than half of new businesses in the UK close within three years of opening their doors. An investment in a start-up can resemble a turn on a roulette wheel. At the same time, those who choose wisely can reap handsome rewards.

If you would like to explore this option, attend a meeting of your regional business development agency and watch the presentations given by entrepreneurs in search of investors. It is like

Dragon's Den, but without the showbiz and posturing – and with hundreds of potential 'Dragons' sitting in the audience. Keep your ear to the ground, so that you can find out about opportunities as they arise. Let other people in your networks know what you are looking for, so that suitable opportunities can find you too.

7. You! Reinvest in yourself. You made the money in the first place, so you have a track record and you represent a sound business proposition. You could:

o fund your pursuit of new Learning Threads, to improve your skill-sets and performance within your chosen field;

o invest in research and development, so that you can launch a new product or service;

o secure an acquisition – ideally, an ailing company in your marketplace – that would expand your business and raise its potential to new heights.

Buyer beware

Approach the following with caution.

o **Financial advisers.** There are some wonderful financial advisers out there, but there are plenty of useless ones too. Many financial and fund managers receive their fees or commission upfront, and will take money from you even if their performance turns out to be below par.

Only hand over your money to someone who clearly cares for it as much as you do. Before appointing financial professionals, research their companies and their track records as thoroughly as you can. If you decide to meet any of them, find out if they put their money where their mouths are. Are they prepared to show you their own portfolios?

○ **Loans to family and friends**. Such loans could be regarded as excellent investment decisions, even though they are unlikely to yield any financial profits. After all, aren't you helping to build strong Family and Relationship Threads when you invest in the futures of those who are dear to you?

In some cases, this is true. In others, loans can end up damaging relationships rather than improving them. Repayment issues and a sense of obligation can lead to resentment and unease.

If a friend or a member of your family approaches you and asks for financial assistance, sit down with them and dig to the bottom of their situation. If you part with any cash, do so after imparting advice; if you hand out sums willy-nilly and without comment, the recipients will learn little. If you do decide to help them out, it is essential that you are able to write off this money, if necessary. Remove the expectation of a return, and you are better-placed to avoid difficulties and tension in the long run.

○ **Depleted reserves**. Don't tie up everything you have in investments. Always keep cash available, preferably enough to cover your living expenses for several months. Prepare for the unexpected.

○ **Putting your money in one place**. This was mentioned in the previous chapter but is worth repeating here because, while the economy remains in turmoil, the perils posed by keeping your wealth together cannot be understated.

The UK Government safeguards all deposits in UK banks to the value of £50,000 at the time of writing. Even so, our times are uncertain and you should not commit large sums of money to a single location.

○ **Pressure**. Don't allow advisers to rush you or push you into anything. Other opportunities will always come your way. If pressure is applied, ask yourself this question: 'Why must I sign today: is it for my benefit or theirs?'

I like to attend financial meetings with my wife Jo. Our Wealth Threads feed into our Family Threads because of the impact they have upon the quality of our family life, so we believe it is important that we are both involved. We only choose options on which we both agree.

I appreciate Jo's input for other reasons too. She is prudent and scrupulous. She asks lots of questions, and always reads terms and conditions very carefully. On a number of occasions Jo has raised the red flag. Recently, for example, we were steered towards a particular financial product and informed that the return on our investment would be guaranteed. But Jo combed through the small print and discovered that this was not the case. In truth, the return was only guaranteed if a range of somewhat ambitious criteria was met in full. We dismissed this product and its seller out of hand.

We aren't pushovers. We are cautious and studious, and we pay a lot of attention to detail. Our own experiences have taught us that these are essential qualities. We want to make our Wealth Threads as strong as they can be.

SUMMARY

● You can strengthen your Wealth Threads and your Golden Rope by sending your surplus income out to work. Earning an income isn't a means to an end; it's a means to a beginning.

● There are few 'one size fits all' opportunities. Different investment options suit different people and carry varying degrees of risk.

● Never risk more than you are prepared to lose.

● For the best results, strengthen your Learning Threads and gather a sound knowledge of the market's products, quirks and pitfalls. The more you know, the more you can do and be.

ACTION POINTS

1. If you don't do this already, begin reading the financial pages in the newspapers. It is a good way to learn about finance and the economy, and to familiarise yourself with market terms and trends. Whenever you come across a phrase or a concept that you do not understand, research it on the internet.

2. Explore the following websites, in preparation for the worksheet (opposite).

www.investopedia.com
www.moneymadeclear.fsa.gov.uk
www.finance.yahoo.com/education

These are all sites that contain useful, impartial information about the various investment options available to you. Also look at comparison sites, such as www.moneysupermarket.com and www.fool.co.uk.

3. Become a member of an organisation that will help you to plan your financial future. Wealth Enhancement Forums, Business Link groups, the Academy for Chief Executives, Vistage International and regional business development groups are good starting points.

If you don't wish to join any of these organisations, take a wealthy person out for coffee. It could be the owner of the business for which you work, a wealthy relative or a neighbour with a paid-for Porsche on the front drive. Ask them about money management. What do they do with their money? How do they put it out to work? How do they make their investment decisions? To whom do they recommend you speak, for further advice?

WORKSHEET

Imagine that you have £5,000 to invest and complete the following table, drawing upon internet resources such as the sites listed above.

This is a research-based exercise. It will ensure that you have a working knowledge of the various options for sending your money out to work, and of the potential advantages and disadvantages of each one.

Example

SAVINGS

Best deal	5-year ROI*
Xxx Building Society are offering an online access account with 2.5% + 1% bnus for 12 months	£5,175

For	Against
Safe haven, attractive interest rate, easy access to my money	Low risk = relatively lower return

ROI means return on investment

SAVINGS

Best deal	5-year ROI

For	Against

PREMIUM BONDS

Best deal   5-year ROI

For   Against

GILT EDGED BONDS

Best deal   5-year ROI

For   Against

GUARANTEED GROWTH BONDS

Best deal   5-year ROI

For   Against

GUARANTEED INCOME BOND

Best deal   5-year ROI

For   Against

CASH ISA

Best deal   5-year ROI

For   Against

EQUITIES ISA

Best deal   5-year ROI

For   Against

PART 4

The Productivity Threads

CHAPTER 10

The most precious resource

A successful life is an accumulation of successful days. Underpinning every successful day is the successful use of time: the ability to complete tasks and fulfil responsibilities within a set period.

Time is fixed and its march is unstoppable. It is also a great leveller: our lives may be at different stages and in different places, but we share the same hours. What you do with those hours and how well you use them is down to you.

66 You don't 'manage time'; you manage the events that occur within that time. 99

The Productivity Threads form a slim but significant section of this book, running through every area of your life. They are an important addition to your Golden Rope.

Having read this far, you will know that *this book* is full of ways to make your life all that it can be and more besides. There is much to do: the mind and body have to be trained, families have to be looked after, and there are valuable relationships that are to be forged and maintained. And that is just for starters! Now that you have more tasks, activities and ambitions to be fitted into your allotted time, how are you going to achieve this?

It doesn't help that here in the UK we are working a greater number of hours every week, compared to previous genera-tions. Single-income families are no longer the norm; in many households, both partners work full time. Our spare time is at a premium.

Too many people end up filling their time, rather than planning it. Work tends to fit into a day as liquid fits into the bottom of a jar: it expands to fit the space that is available. Productivity Threads will become weakened when minutes and hours that could have been put to better use are frittered away. Once time has gone, there's no clawing it back.

You will find when you are enthusiastic about the tasks ahead, or when your in-tray is overflowing, your productivity soars. Even when your time is limited, you somehow manage to fit everything in. This shows that when you are excited about what you are doing, you have the ability to manage your activities wonderfully well.

Begin tapping into that ability on a daily basis and good activity management will become an ingrained habit.

The Golden Threads life journal

The page from Marc's *Golden Threads Life Journal* (overleaf) shows how a busy day can be carefully planned and managed, so that maximum value is extracted from the time available.

Even when Marc's day is thrown into disarray by unexpected events, he can see at a glance the tasks that have yet to be completed, and can reschedule them with the minimum of fuss.

The *Golden Threads Life Journal* isn't just for work: Marc also schedules his fitness regime, holidays and family time.

Twelve strides to better activity management

1. Purchase a good quality diary, into which you can write your goals, activities and tasks for the coming days and weeks. It is an essential tool for organising your life as efficiently as possible. A page-a-day diary from a stationery shop is suitable. Alternatively, you can purchase a copy of the *Golden Threads Life Journal*; this is a hardback book that has been carefully tailored to meet your needs. The journal enables you to break down your 'to do' list, prioritise your tasks and incorporate your long-term goals. It is available to order from www.yourgoldenthreads.com

NOTES, CALLS & REMINDERS

YOUR GOLDEN THREADS FOR THE WEEK

	MONDAY	TUESDAY	WEDNESDAY	THURSDAY	FRIDAY	SATURDAY
am						

						SUNDAY
pm						

2. Work your plan. Make a point of dispatching tasks as they are planned – not as they land. Don't let yourself be thrown off course by non-urgent items. Scan through your e-mails every morning, and schedule the periods of time in which you will reply to the important items. That way, you can avoid becoming bogged down in the non-urgent tasks and correspondence that stream in during the course of the day.

3. If a job's worth doing, it's worth doing well. Don't cut corners or opt for temporary fixes. Instead, search out permanent solutions that will save you time in the long run. So if your boiler keeps breaking down, don't keep whacking it until it wheezes into life again. If a 'repair' is short-term, you are only making more work for yourself in the long term. Pay someone to mend it properly.

4. Plan in advance. There's a reason why 'fail to plan, and you plan to fail' has become a well-used phrase. Don't wait until the morning to allocate your tasks for that day. Do it the day before. If you arrive at work with your plan already in place, you can get stuck into that day without further ado. Likewise if you have young children, don't wait until morning to lay out their clothes and make their packed lunches.

Plan in advance so that whenever a new day begins, it is already finished on paper.

66 A new day should be finished on paper before it begins. 99

5. Exercise regularly. See the Health Threads section for exercise tips, plans and beginners' programmes. When you are fit and healthy, your concentration levels are raised. Your productivity is increased, because you have increased your energy levels and can work for longer periods without tiring.

6. Get up half an hour earlier every morning. Get more from your day by getting up earlier and filling that recouped time with exercise. You shouldn't feel tired: as you become fitter, the amount of sleep that you need will decrease. If you do feel tired, continue getting up at this new time, but begin going to bed half an hour earlier.

7. Don't skip meals, but have light lunches. Eat fresh fruit and make yourself salads for lunch. During the day, avoid carbohydrate-rich foods such as bread, pasta, potatoes or large pieces of meat. If you work outside the home, take your homemade salad with you. Heavy lunches can make you tired and sluggish in the afternoon; light, healthy lunches will help you to stay awake and alert.

8. Keep moving ahead. Study your work, and explore ways of boosting your abilities to manage activities effectively. For example, if you notice that a colleague's productivity levels have soared, ask them how they did it. View this as an exercise in continuous improvement.

9. Go the extra mile. This applies to everyone. If you work in sales or if your work is customer-facing, aim to make one more call a day than anyone else in your team. Little by little, this small extra effort will accumulate results and make you more effective at what you do. If you are a full-time homemaker, make twice as much food and deep freeze half of it to slash the time that you spend preparing meals.

10. Delegate! The art of delegation should not be underestimated, as it will free up your time and allow you to fit more into your day. It applies to the home as well as the office: if you have children, give them regular chores such as hanging out the washing and laying the table for dinner.

A note of warning: don't use your powers of delegation to opt out of unpleasant or tiresome tasks, or to dole out tasks to people who aren't equipped to take them on. If your delegation fails and becomes unpopular with those around you, your autocratic working style may eventually cost you more time than it saves.

11. Wherever you are, be there. Stay on plan and don't allow distractions to take over your day. Concentrate on doing what you are there to do. If people keep calling you about non-essential matters, turn your mobile phone off. If you find yourself aimlessly surfing the internet when you have more important things to do or deadlines to meet, go offline until your deadlines have been met.

12. Finally: fill your days with treasures, not trinkets. Make every day worth remembering. Aim to achieve something new, day in, day out. This could be anything, from landing a lucrative new business contract to learning a new word. Write the day's achievement into your journal before you go to bed. This will help ensure a restful night's sleep.

66 Never meet anyone in person that could be dealt with on the phone or email 99

SUMMARY

○ Activity management is the ability to complete tasks and fulfil responsibilities within fixed periods of time.

○ Fail to plan and you plan to fail. Too many people end up filling their time, rather than planning it. Productivity Threads will be weakened by minutes and hours that have been frittered away, when they could have been put to better use.

○ A *Golden Threads Life Journal,* or a page-a-day diary, is an essential time management tool that will send your productivity skywards.

WORKSHEET

The table below breaks up one day into slots of 30 minutes apiece. Pick a day from the coming week and fill out this time sheet with all the activities that you undertake as the hours pass, following the printed examples. (If the time sheet does not fit your waking hours, please amend the times.)

The next morning, review your completed table. What did you achieve? Would you say that overall, your day was productive? How much of your time did you use wisely? Identify areas for improvement.

Example

TIME	ACTIVITY	PRODUCTIVE?
0630–0700	Asleep	Yes
0700–0730	Hitting the snooze button on my alarm clock instead of going for a run	No
0730–0800	Getting ready for work and getting the kids out of bed	Yes
0800–0830		
0830–0900		
0900–0930		
0930–1000		
1000–1030		
1030–1100		
1100–1130		
1130–1200		

1200–1230		
1230–1300		
1300–1330		
1330–1400		
1400–1430		
1430–1500		
1500–1530		
1530–1600		
1600–1630		
1630–1700		
1700–1730		
1730–1800		
1800–1830		
1830–1900		
1900–1930		
1930–2000		
2000–2030		
2030–2100		

ACTION POINTS

You may have noticed that the usual order of the action points and worksheet has been reversed in this chapter. This is so that once you have identified any shortcomings in your one-day time sheet, you can take the following actions to ensure that they are not repeated.

1. Go to www.yourgoldenthreads.com, download the sample page of the *Golden Threads Life Journal* and print it out.

2. Write tomorrow's date at the top, then fill the blank journal page with as much detail as possible. Schedule everything that you plan to achieve tomorrow. By putting your objectives on paper and allocating specific times and slots, you are more likely to carry out these tasks at the appointed times.

3. If your completed worksheet showed that some of your time could have been used more wisely, make a point of filling your journal from top to bottom. For example, if you are in the habit of aimlessly surfing the internet after your lunch every day, be sure to schedule a demanding activity in its place.

4. What tasks have you have been putting off? Include at least two in your journal. Also aim to include at least one social activity; this could be anything from a dinner out to standing at the school gate with the other parents.

PART 5

The Health
Threads

CHAPTER 11

ealth matters

A Golden Thread on its own is fragile and can easily be broken; however, a mass of Golden Threads, bound together into a strong rope, is unbreakable.

This section explores the various ways in which improvements to your eating habits and to your exercise regime can enrich other areas of your life, by creating the time, space and energy for new possibilities and projects.

The Health Threads run through every area of your life. It follows that when the quality of your health improves, so does every other thread in your life.

 Nothing tastes like fit feels.

What is 'good health'?

In our everyday lives we are surrounded by confusing, sometimes conflicting messages about what we should be doing to stay healthy. Magazines and newspapers are filled with celebrity weight loss stories and articles about so-called 'superfoods'. The television schedules are dominated by 'makeover experts'. Exercise DVDs are bestsellers, and shelves in shops and libraries are stuffed full of guides to healthy eating.

So, just to make it clear, this is what good health is not:

- The preserve of po-faced television 'gurus'. Good health can be studied and enjoyed by everyone.
- Accelerated exercise plans, which dangle impossible promises. Do you really believe that you are going to be 'beach fit in just four weeks'?
- Restrictive, low-calorie diets that take the enjoyment out of eating.

- Sparkling eyes and shiny hair. These are the outward signs of good health, but they can be easily faked. It is how you feel on the inside that is more important.
- 'Offsetting' a party lifestyle with lots of exercise.

This last point may sound confusing to some readers. After all, if you keep fit and your body is strong, then surely you are a healthy person?

Marc knew a man who worked as a PE instructor in the British Army. This man belonged to the trampoline team, the boxing team, the gymnastics team and the swimming team. Without any training or preparation, he once ran the Berlin Marathon in fewer than four hours. He was exceptionally fit, but his eating habits were atrocious. He lived on fast food, smoked at least 20 cigarettes a day and drank to excess. He shunned fruit and vegetables. Despite his physical prowess, he was the unhealthiest individual that Marc has known. After this man left the army, his health – and his quality of life – entered a swift decline.

A good level of fitness contributes to your state of health, but it doesn't define it.

Good health is about feeling good, rather than looking good. A lot of people focus upon the latter, but looking good is a by-product of good health. Simply put, good health is a state of continual alertness and wellness. It's the result of four factors: the right eating habits, the right fitness, the right amount of rest and the right mindset.

If you have worked through the Learning Threads section of this book, you will already have the right mindset in place. Now let's set to work.

Why good health is important

Does the following sound familiar?

- You sleep through your alarm and get up late.
- After coughing up your lungs, you have a quick shower and pull on odd socks.
- You gulp down a cup of scalding coffee, spilling some of it down your clothes. Still, at least you have 'come alive'!
- Stuck in traffic, you remember that you have forgotten important documents. Your car is low on fuel, but you are running late and don't have time to fill it.
- You are already stressed and anxious before you have even arrived at work.

If your mornings are like this, the good news is that you have bought the right book. It is time to get back behind the controls. Imagine feeling 50 per cent better than you feel at this moment. How much more could you do and how much more could you handle? How much more could you earn? How much more could you give to yourself and to your loved ones?

Scientists have concluded that physical activity has the same effect as antidepressants. It stimulates neurotransmitters in our brain to produce endorphins, which are chemicals that create a sense of well-being. There is also emerging evidence suggesting that dietary phytochemicals (compounds that occur naturally in plant-based foods), in particular flavonoids, may be capable of improving memory and learning. Flavonoids are found naturally in foods such as fruits, vegetables, cereals, tea, wine and fruit juices.

It has also been suggested that certain additives in food, including some artificial colourings, can adversely affect behaviour, attention and concentration. This has only been demonstrated in children, however, and may only affect a relatively small proportion of children. Even so, most food manufacturers have now removed all artificial colourings and flavourings from their food.

A good diet not only helps to enhance general well-being and maintain a healthy body weight, but also reduces the risk of diseases, including heart disease, stroke, cancer, diabetes and osteoporosis. In a report by the Cabinet Office, published in 2008, it was estimated that 69,400 people in the UK die every year because of poor diet. This is one in ten of all deaths.

You don't have to look hard to find information about diet and health. In fact, it can seem that every time you open a newspaper or magazine you are told what you should eat, or not eat. The information can be confusing, because much of it can appear to be contradictory, but this does not have to be the case. The advice in the Health Threads will give you all the tools and knowledge to help you to lead a long and healthy life.

Good health has a positive effect on every aspect of life, around the clock. If you enjoy good health you sleep well. You wake up refreshed, renewed and ready to start the day. Because you are full of energy, you get up on time and begin work 15 minutes early.

As you go about your work you have a bounce in your step, a smile on your face and a 'glow' that others will notice. You walk with confidence, as though you are on a mission. That gets others' attention, too. You aren't testy or short-tempered. Because you feel good, you want to do good. People are drawn to you.

To reach and maintain this state of good health isn't always easy. It requires discipline and commitment. But when you can build this discipline, the benefits also spill over into other areas of your life.

Stamp out the excuses

We are all creatures of habit. Unfortunately, it is very easy to get into bad habits – and it takes much more effort to get into good ones. It follows that the things that are worth having require a greater amount of effort; often, the things that are easy to get are worth little.

Here are some common excuses from people who shirk efforts to improve their health.

● **Healthy eating habits and exercise aren't my 'thing'**. If you aren't convinced of the benefits of healthy eating and exercise, this is because you have rarely experienced them. Games at school don't count! Transform your health for the better, and you will feel wonderful.

● **I can't afford to eat well/keep fit**. The following chapters will demonstrate that this simply isn't true.

● **I can't do any exercise because of my medical condition**. Your condition may mean that any exercise plan requires expert input from your GP or another relevant medical professional, but it should be possible to put some sort of plan together. Remember Leeds mother Jane Tomlinson? Jane had been diagnosed with terminal cancer, but decided that her condition would not stop her from completing a series of athletic challenges for charity. She completed the London Marathon three times, the London Triathlon twice and the New York Marathon once. She cycled across Europe, the United States and Africa. If Jane Tomlinson could do all of this while coping with a terminal condition, can't you find a way to exercise in spite of your own medical challenges?

● **Life is for living**. Exactly: that's why you can't put a price on good health. Don't sell yourself short, or look for happiness at the bottom of a bottle or with drugs. Physical exercise and good nutrition will give you more life to live; no short-term chemical high can ever give you the long-term benefits of a natural high. We know that substance abuse creates havoc within families and society. If this is something that affects you personally, seek help sooner rather than later. Contact Addaction, the UK's biggest drugs and alcohol treatment charity, on 020 7251 5890, or visit www.addaction.org.uk

If you smoke and you wish to give up, plenty of help is available. Your doctor will be able to advise you on your options; alternatively, visit www.smokefree.nhs.uk for further information.

○ **My granddad lived until he was 94 – and he drank like a fish and smoked like a chimney**. This may be true, but exceptions are not the rule. You forgot to add that, unlike you, he walked four miles to work and back every day, never ate junk food and was in bed by 8 pm every night.

○ **I have big bones, I weigh heavy**. There are different human physical types, ranging from ectomorph (narrow) to endomorph (wider). However, excess of body fat is associated with an adverse health risk, most notably an increased risk of heart disease, type 2 diabetes, and some forms of cancer. And even if you are 'big boned', why would that prevent you from becoming healthier?

○ **I have a manual job**. Nope, not good enough. While some manual workers enjoy rude health, others do not. They may have strong, muscular arms from all the physical labour, but the core of good health is the heart, which is at the centre of your cardiovascular system. A healthy heart is the result of aerobic exercise and healthy eating habits.

○ **I'm too old**. Really? The oldest person to complete the London Marathon was 101; the 2008 Olympics featured several athletes in their sixth and seventh decades. You are only as old as you feel.

What is there to be gained by postponing your own well-being?

At 65, I feel that I am in the prime of my life. I can't remember the last day I went down with a bug, or had to spend the day in bed because I wasn't feeling well. Unfortunately some people in their sixties think that yoga is something they put on their muesli, and that putting on their socks without assistance counts as exercise.

I still go to the gym on a regular basis, and keeping myself amused is important to me. If a young buck is following me around the gym, when I move on from a machine I sometimes take care to move the weight pin 30 or 40 kilos heavier than I used. I do this discreetly. Then I watch the younger man goggle at me as he struggles with the weights he thinks the old guy just lifted before him! I am physically active because I like to be mentally active. I am mentally active because I love the buzz of life and day-to-day business. I can't imagine my life any other way.

Feel and live the benefits

The following two chapters cover eating habits and exercise in greater detail. Are you prepared to develop new, healthy habits that will improve your mind, increase your productivity and make you healthier and happier? If you are, then read on.

When you think your best thoughts and take your best actions, you will find that your positive efforts spill over into the rest of your life. Once you begin, you'll never look back.

SUMMARY

- Good health is a state of continual alertness and wellness.

- Improvements to your health will enrich other areas of your life, by creating the time and space for new possibilities and projects.

- To reach and maintain a state of good health requires discipline and commitment.

ACTION POINTS

1. Know your numbers. Cardiovascular specialist Dr Dorian Dugmore, Director of the Wellness Centre at adidas (UK) Ltd (www. wellnessinternational.co.uk), has found that wellness and longevity can be pinned down to some simple numbers. Memorise the numbers below and check them regularly.

○ **72.** This is your resting heart rate, measured first thing in the morning or after you have been sat down for some time. Seventy-two is the number of times that the average heart beats in one minute, but generally speaking the lower this number, the better. (As long as it's above zero!)

○ **140/85.** This is your blood pressure. If your blood pressure rises above this number you may have hypertension, which can lead to strokes and heart attacks. If you need to, you may be able to lower your blood pressure by reducing your salt intake, increasing the amount of exercise you take, revamping your eating regime to include plenty of fruit and vegetables and reducing the amount of 'bad' saturated fats (such as dairy products) that you consume. You can ask your GP to take your blood pressure, or you can purchase a blood pressure monitor from your local pharmacist.

○ **14–20.** This is your body fat percentage: the mass of your body fat, as a percentage of your overall weight. Ideally this number should fall somewhere between 14 and 20. You can measure your body fat percentage at a gym, using callipers. Alternatively, you can assess it using scales that measure body fat as well as body mass. These work by a principle known as bioelectrical impedance analysis (BIA). These scales can be bought for home use and are available from retailers such as www.bathroom-trends.co.uk for around £20.

Healthy body fat ranges vary by age and also sex. The average man has between 15 and 17 per cent body fat, while the average woman has between 18 and 22 per cent. When body fat percentage is above 20 for a male, and above 30 for a female, it can be lowered by a sensible, healthy eating regime in combination with a sound exercise programme. The following chart shows you what a healthy body fat percentage should be for you:

SEX	AGE	BODY FAT PERCENTAGE
Male	20–39	8–20
	40–59	11–22
	60–79	13–25
Female	20–39	21–33
	40–59	23–34
	60–79	24–36

○ **18.5–24.9**. This is what a 'healthy' body mass index (BMI) should be. Those with a BMI above 25 are classed as overweight, while those with a BMI above 30 are classed as obese. Those classed as obese have an increased risk of developing conditions such as heart disease, certain cancers and type 2 diabetes. The BMI is calculated by dividing your weight in kilograms by your height in metres. In essence, it is a measure of whether you are carrying too much weight for your height. You can calculate your BMI by using the online calculators at www.yourgoldenthreads.com; alternatively, your doctor can calculate your BMI for you.

○ **5.0 mmol/l**. This is the number for your total cholesterol. An awareness of your cholesterol level will help you improve and maintain the condition of your heart. It is generally accepted that a cholesterol figure of less than 5.0 mmol/l is ideal for heart health, but around 67 per cent of healthy men and women aged between 16 and 75 have a blood cholesterol level of 5.0 mmol/l or above. Be warned: a high cholesterol level is a risk factor for heart disease. Around 56 per cent of cases of coronary heart disease can be attributed to raised cholesterol levels. Please note that if you have cardiovascular disease, you are advised to have a total cholesterol level of less than 4.0 mmol/l.

It is also important to know what your 'good' and 'bad' cholesterol levels are. The good cholesterol, known as high-density lipoprotein (HDL), is called 'good' cholesterol because it transports cholesterol from body tissues to the liver, where it is used to produce bile or excreted. Low levels of HDL cholesterol are associated with an increased risk of coronary heart disease.

The other type of cholesterol is low-density lipoprotein (LDL). This is known as 'bad' cholesterol because it transports cholesterol from the liver to the body tissues. 'Bad' cholesterol gets deposited in the walls of our arteries, which can cause them to narrow.

If you would like to find out your cholesterol level, your GP can measure this for you. There are also a number of home testing kits on the market, although these may not be as accurate as a test performed by your doctor.

Some time ago I had my heart rate tested by a cardiologist. My resting heart rate was 43 beats per minute. Not bad! The average resting heart rate is 72 beats per minute, and my relatively low number of beats showed that my heart was strong. I felt pleased with myself.

However, I then discovered that my body fat percentage was 20.3 per cent. Someone of my age and weight should have a body fat percentage of between 14 per cent and 20 per cent. Then I learned that my level of LDL cholesterol was 4.57, when it should have been below 3. Not so good after all, eh?

My point is simple: you should not assume that because one of your numbers is good, you have strong Health Threads. Good health and wellness are the composite result of a number of factors. Keep your eye on all of them.

2. Take your waist measurement. Many people – men in particular – think they are fitter than they are, and underestimate their size. So guess your waist measurement, then take a tape measure and find out if the reality matches your expectation. If it doesn't, take heart: at least if you know where you are starting from, you are in a much better position to do something about it. In general, men are at increased risk of obesity-related diseases when their waist circumference reaches 94 cm (37 inches). For women, risks increase at 80 cm (32 inches). The risks of disease become substantially increased at 102 cm (40 inches) for men and 88 cm (35 inches) for women.

3. Seek advice if necessary. If you have a medical condition or you have been feeling unwell, it is imperative that you seek advice from your GP before you begin a new healthy eating regime or exercise programme.

WORKSHEET

If you don't know how to measure your resting heart rate, now is the time to learn. After sitting and relaxing for at least 10 minutes, take off your watch and place it in front of you. Press your right forefinger and middle finger upon your left wrist. Find your pulse on the tendon closest to the left thumb, just by the bone that runs down from the thumb. Looking at your watch, count the beats over 15 seconds. Then multiply by four, to get your resting heart rate per minute.

Over the next year, on the same day of every month, measure your resting heart rate and enter it into the following table:

MONTH	HEART RATE
1	
2	
3	
4	
5	
6	
7	
8	
9	
10	
11	
12	

As you become healthier, your resting heart rate should fall. Your heart is a muscle, which is strengthened through exercise. When your heart becomes stronger, it requires less effort to pump blood around your body. Imagine how your health will benefit if your heart rate slows by five beats a minute. That amounts to 7,200 beats per day. Over a year, you would save 2,628,000 beats. Not only can this saving add years to your life, it will also add life to your years. Make a habit of monitoring your resting heart rate on a regular basis.

CHAPTER 12

Thought for food

L ife is complicated enough without having to follow complex and intricate eating plans. Yet many of the most popular diets and fads revolve around a mind-boggling array of theories, rules, balances, points, principles, charts, timetables, arithmetic and unpalatable food combinations. It is as if the more 'clever' the plan, the more 'scientific' and effective that plan must be. Plans are peddled as miracle answers; many people see them as clever solutions that do away with the need to make necessary lifestyle adjustments.

People who settle for detailed, prescribed diets tend to be looking for quick fixes. Some people may be seeking to lose weight; others may be hoping for six-packs. In reality, quick fixes are nothing of the kind. The 'cabbage soup diet' can work wonders while you're on it – but are you going to eat nothing but cabbage soup for the rest of your life?

You may have come across all sorts of weird and wonderful-sounding diets out there, all promising miracle results. Many 'fad' diets work in principle, because they dictate a dietary regime of fewer than 500 calories per day. If you consume less calories than you require on a daily basis, you will lose weight. For many, however, this weight loss does not last. Such drastic diets can also be dangerous, leaving their followers feeling fatigued, dizzy, light-headed and downright awful. If these types of diets are so beneficial, why have rates of obesity quadrupled in the past 25 years? Some research suggests that 95 per cent of slimmers regain the weight they lose. The diet industry in the UK is worth an estimated £1 billion a year, but does it rely on our failure to make its profits?

In reality, there is no such thing as a quick fix. A change to your eating and shopping habits can only be effective in the long term if it is a permanent change. For many people, losing weight will be one of the greatest challenges they face. Some fail because they try to change everything in their life at once. The best way to succeed is to begin by making two or three changes that you can stick to, then taking it from there. Over time, you'll see the results.

66 Small changes to your shopping list will bring about big benefits in a short space of time. 99

This chapter is dedicated to healthy eating for improved wellness, but it is not a turbo-charged weight loss programme. Nor is it a complex dietary regime to be followed with military efficiency. Diet sheets and meal plans are not provided.

Instead, we'll give you a list of simple but effective eating habits which are easily achieved and inexpensive. We know they work because they have already helped thousands of people that we've worked with to feel better inside and out.

The guidelines centre upon one principle, and one principle only: that the better you feel, the more you will achieve. If you are what you eat, it follows that by improving what you eat, you can improve who you are and what you are capable of doing.

Are you ready to transform your eating habits? Then let's begin.

1. **Limit what you eat out of packets**. Look in your cupboards: if they are full of foods such as processed meats, cakes, biscuits, sweets and soft drinks, it is time to rethink your shopping list. Try to eat fresh food as much as possible. If you can't pronounce an ingredient on the back of a food packet, avoid it!

2. **Take your time with every mouthful**, rather than gulping your food down. Doesn't it seem strange that you'll see people in city centres striding purposefully while they are eating their fast food lunch – but 10 minutes later they'll be in the park, relaxing while they smoke their cigarettes? Take your time and not only will you enjoy your meals all the more, but also your body will be able to digest the food more easily.

3. **Limit the amount of red meat that you eat**. Avoid or limit your consumption of fatty cuts of meat such as marbled rump steak, pork chops on the bone, bacon and processed meat products such as luncheon meat, salami and sausages. There is some evidence that too much red meat and processed meats can increase your risk of cancer. Choose lean cuts such as skinless chicken or turkey breast.

4. **Eat small amounts on a regular basis during the day**, so that you won't feel the need to snack on sweets and biscuits. A mid-morning snack could be an apple, orange and banana; a mid-afternoon snack could be some nuts, raisins or a muesli bar. Eating small, regular meals throughout the day stops you snacking on unhealthy snacks and can also help with losing weight.

5. Big, stodgy meals will make you feel sleepy, so **stop eating when you begin to feel full**. Overeating can be a hard habit to break, but learning to recognise the full feeling is key to maintaining a healthy body weight. One of the easiest ways to do this is to limit your portion size. You could also use a smaller plate. On your plate, have a palm-sized portion of meat or fish and a palm-sized portion of carbohydrates such as potatoes or rice. The rest of the plate should be filled with vegetables or salad. If you feel hungry afterwards, live with it for a while.

6. Count on yourself, but **never count on counting**. Calories are important to many people who are trying to lose weight, but don't count mouthfuls or the number of times that each mouthful is chewed. Eating well isn't about mathematics; it's about choosing the right foods, and being able to sit back and enjoy them.

7. **Put a bag of fruit and a bottle of water in the car** before lengthy car journeys, family outings or at the beginning of the

week. You can get hungry or bored when you are driving distances or stuck in traffic jams, but having a good selection of fruit available means that you won't snack on crisps, or stop off for a fast-food snack and fizzy drink.

8.   **Don't eat your children's leftovers**. You aren't a pedal bin.

9.   Choose cooking methods that require **the least amount of fat or oil**, such as grilling, baking or steaming. Avoid fried foods.

10. **Eat plenty of fibre-rich foods**. Fibre is an important part of any healthy eating regime. It makes you feel full and aids digestion by slowing the absorption of sugars into your blood. Fruits and vegetables are high fibre foods. Nuts, seeds, brown rice, beans and wholemeal bread are also fibre-rich. An eating regime that is rich in fibre can help to prevent constipation, lower blood cholesterol levels, control blood glucose levels, reduce the risk of bowel cancer and aid weight loss. Fibre-rich foods fill you up and keep you feeling fuller for longer. Research has also indicated that people who eat high fibre diets tend to be slimmer.

11. **Replace full-fat milk with skimmed or semi-skimmed**. In fact, you may wish to reconsider your dairy intake. An increasingly popular school of thought argues that dairy products are bad for us. Research has linked cow's milk to conditions ranging from acne to diabetes. Moreover, our recommended daily calcium can be readily obtained from other foodstuffs such as spinach and broccoli. Visit www.milkmyths.org.uk (which argues that milk may not be good for us) and www.milk.co.uk (which argues for milk's health benefits) and make up your own mind.

12. **Limit your intake of sweet pastries and cakes**. If you crave them, eat a piece of fresh fruit instead. There are many different

fruits available; these days, even supermarkets sell exotic and unusual varieties. If you are in a restaurant, the same rule applies: fruit salads are usually available as a dessert option.

13. Keep an eye on how much saturated fat you are consuming. This is because saturated fat can increase the level of LDL cholesterol, which can increase your risk of heart disease. The over-consumption of saturated fats in the UK is of particular concern as 88% of British men and 83% of British women eat more than the guidelines recommend. Foods that are high in saturated fat include lard, ghee, butter, cream, pastries, fried foods, fatty cuts of meat, cakes and biscuits.

It is recommended that we consume a maximum of 20g of saturated fat each day. This amount of saturated fat can be found in each of the following:

- An individual steak and kidney pie.
- A cappuccino and a Danish pastry.
- Two sausages and two individual butter portions.
- One slice of pizza, a glass of full-fat milk and a portion of chips.
- A croissant, followed by a cheese sandwich with butter and a shortbread finger.
- Three rashers of streaky bacon, two lamb chops and a chocolate-covered biscuit bar.
- One hot chocolate with cream, one jam doughnut, one bag of crisps and three small squares of chocolate.

14. Always eat breakfast: studies have shown that skipping breakfast has a negative effect on performance at school and work. But swap processed breakfast cereal, which is often high in sugar, for additive-free muesli such as Dorset Cereals and others, which are packed with nuts, seeds and dried fruits. A 2003 study found that children who breakfasted on high-sugar foods and drinks had the memory skills and attention spans of 70-year-olds. If you are not used to having breakfast, try having something light such as a glass of freshly-squeezed orange juice, a smoothie, a slice of toast, a small bowl of cereal or a low-fat yoghurt. These are all foods that are generally well tolerated in the morning, and are not very heavy on the stomach.

Aim to eat at least two portions of fish each week. At least one of these portions should be oily fish such as wild salmon, mackerel or tuna. They are rich in essential fats called omega-3 fatty acids, which help maintain a healthy heart. It has also been suggested that fish omega-3 has the potential to affect mood, behaviour, mental health and memory, although these theories have yet to be confirmed. Finally, omega-3 from fish has been linked to the improvement of inflammatory conditions such as arthritis.

15. Eat plenty of fruit and vegetables. Have them for a snack, or as a dessert. Slice them and add them to your breakfast muesli, instead of sugar. Fruit and vegetables give you plenty of vitamins and minerals. They are also a good source of fibre. Eat as many raw vegetables as you can. Cut them up and serve them as snacks.

16. Don't overcook vegetables. Boiling vegetables breaks down some of their vitamins. The best way to keep as much of the water-soluble vitamins as possible is to steam, grill or microwave, rather than boil. If you do boil your vegetables, don't add salt to the cooking water.

17. Pulses (such as beans and lentils) are high in protein, which maintains and repairs bone, tissue, organs and blood. It is also used to make your brain's neurotransmitters. Think about ways to **introduce more pulses into your food regime**. Add them to soups, serve them as side dishes, or use instead of meat in dishes.

Protein-rich foods also can have a role to play in weight loss as they make you feel fuller for longer. But remember: foods high in protein should be eaten in moderation. A high-protein diet may damage vital organs such as liver and kidneys.

18. If you crave a chocolate fix, have a chocolate fix. But add value by having something else with it, such as fresh fruit. Go for high quality dark chocolate, which is high in flavonols (a class of flavonoid). There is growing evidence that flavonols can change a number of processes associated with cardiovascular disease; these chemicals have also been shown to have a positive effect on the brain. Chocolate, and products containing it, often have relatively high amounts of fat and sugar and should be eaten in moderation. Choose chocolate that contains at least 70 per cent cocoa butter.

19. Drink lots of water. When dehydrated, your brain does not work at full capacity. Try to avoid drinking fluids with meals, as this slows down the digestive process; if you find you have to drink 'to get the food down', you really need to review what you are eating. If your plate of food has a high water content and you chew the food well, why would you need to flush it down? Drink plenty of water in between meals; this habit will also help to stave off hunger. Throughout the day you should be aiming to drink six to eight glasses. If you do a lot of exercise or you sweat a lot, you may wish to drink more than this.

20. Reduce the amount of salt that you consume. It has been shown that a diet high in salt or sodium can lead to an increase in blood pressure (hypertension), which substantially increases the risk of developing heart disease or stroke. Some 75 per cent of an average person's dietary salt intake comes from processed foods; 15–25 per cent comes from the salt that we add.

Many of us sprinkle salt on our food out of habit, rather than necessity. When you reduce your salt intake you will notice that the less salt you eat, the more salt you will be able to taste in your food. If your food tastes bland, don't add more salt – add a squeeze of lemon juice instead. Food writer Sybil Kapoor says that because saltiness is masked by sweetness and enhanced by bitterness and sourness, lemon juice can make salt taste stronger. Use herbs and spices to bring out the flavour of your food. Ready meals, fast food and products that come in tins are often high in salt, so one effective way to reduce your salt intake is to prepare your meals at home.

21. Avoid voids. Every item removed from your plate or dish should be replaced with something else. Instead of a bag of crisps, opt for a bag of mixed nuts and raisins. If you have chips with every meal, opt for a fresh salad instead.

22. Remember that **food preparation and mealtimes should be enjoyable experiences**. Prepare your food in advance, experiment with different dishes and make the most of the mealtimes spent with your family, at the table and away from the television.

S U M M A R Y

- Diets don't have lasting effects because they are temporary in nature. An effective diet is one that you can stick to. You enjoy it, but it doesn't take over your life. A change in your eating and shopping habits can only be effective in the long term if it is a permanent change.

- Good, healthy eating habits are inexpensive and are easy to follow.

- Eating healthily should not feel like a prison sentence. Healthy foods don't have to be bland, and can be just as flavoursome as their fat and calorie-laden counterparts.

- If you are what you eat, it follows that by changing what you eat, you can become a different person.

ACTION POINTS

1. Read through the above list carefully, then take your house-hold's most recent food shopping receipt. With a marker pen, highlight every item that doesn't fit these guidelines. Keep this receipt somewhere safe, as you will need it later.

2. Go through your fridge and cupboards, pulling out all the products that are ill-suited to your new, Golden Threads lifestyle. Give them away or throw them away – but get them out of your kitchen as soon as possible.

3. Empty your biscuit tins. Fill them with fruit or healthy snacks.

4. Always keep a filled fruit bowl on display in your house. Help yourself to its contents, and encourage your family to do the same. When children run out of the house in the morning and grab snacks to take with them, apples or bananas are preferable to packets of salt and vinegar crisps, wouldn't you say?

5. After following the guidelines for one month, take your family's most recent food shopping receipt. With your marker pen, highlight every item that doesn't fit the guidelines. Set it side-by-side with the receipt from the previous month, and compare the two. Note how far you have come, and how much better you all feel.

WORKSHEET

Following the example in the first row of the table, list five products that you have removed from your cupboards or from your eating regime, together with five replacements or new foods that are now on your shopping list.

	OUT WITH THE OLD	IN WITH THE NEW
	Sugar-coated cornflakes	Organic muesli
1		
2		
3		
4		
5		

CHAPTER

13

Fit for life

Exercise improves your brain as well as your body. Studies have shown that people who get regular aerobic exercise are able to learn faster, think more clearly and remember a greater amount. They are less likely to suffer from depression or dementia.

This is because, when you exercise, your brain releases endorphins: hormones that act as painkillers, and produce feelings of euphoria. They give you a natural high. Even moderate amounts of exercise can raise your endorphin levels.

It may be that you already exercise regularly, or attend your local gym. If this is the case, then congratulations: you are building a strong Golden Thread and it will serve you well as you seek to improve your life. Keep it up, and that thread will become stronger still.

If you do not go to the gym or exercise regularly, this chapter is dedicated to you. The following pages set out all you need to know so that you can begin making a big difference to your life.

Get into the habit of exercising regularly, and you'll discover that the benefits extend far beyond your abs, or your heart rate.

When you are physically fit, you feel like a new you.

 Emotion creates motion.

You feel awake and alert, your mood is lifted and you can fit more into your working day. In short, your potential to achieve is greatly expanded.

Five fitness myths

1.   I need to join a gym. It must be said, gym membership comes highly recommended. The facilities and subscription fees provide welcome motivation and, when you are there, the distractions are few. You can also socialise with like-minded people. But if you don't like gyms or don't want to join one for other reasons, you can easily get fit on your own.

2. Everyone gets middle-aged spread, don't they? Not true. A distended abdomen is not a 'natural' state.

3. I don't have time. If this is a sticking point for you, please read the chapter on the Productivity Threads before you do anything else. It will help you to find more time in your day, no matter how busy you are.

Furthermore, improvements to your overall level of health have a snowball effect. The more healthy you become, the less easily you will tire and the more time you will have available.

4. I go to the gym twice a week, so that's me sorted. Twice a week won't make you fitter; it will keep you as you are. If you are hoping to improve your fitness, you will make progress if you go to the gym at least three times a week. The ideal? Five or six visits per week.

5. I'm not important enough. If you have a large family or a stressful occupation, it is tempting and easy to put your needs below those of others. However, if you look after yourself you will be in a position to look after other people and your other priorities all the better. Put your good health at the top of your list, and many other things will fall into place. Make yourself number one, and everyone will benefit.

Strength to Strength programmes for beginners

Here are some suggestions for easy programmes to get you started on your new exercise regime.

Strength to Strength playing card workout

All you need for this are the following:

- A pack of playing cards.
- Comfortable, loose clothes. Designer tracksuits aren't necessary!
- A carpeted floor, or a gym mat.
- Pencil and paper.
- A watch, so that you can time yourself.

The beauty of the Strength to Strength playing card workout is that it costs nothing and you can do it anywhere. No specialist equipment is necessary (unless you have to buy a pack of cards) and no previous experience is required. You can do it at home, if you are working late in the office, or even in your hotel room if you are away.

1. Find a space.

2. Shuffle the cards and lay the pack face down.

3. On your piece of paper, write down the suits on the left-hand side: hearts, clubs, spades and diamonds.

4. Choose one exercise for each suit. For example, you could pair diamonds with press-ups, clubs with star jumps, spades with crunches and hearts with running up and down the stairs. Other exercises could include skipping and running on the spot.

5. Turn over the card on the top of the pack. Which suit is it? The suit you see represents the exercise that you will now do for 30 seconds. So if you have allocated crunches to spades and you have turned over a spade, do crunches for 30 seconds. Time yourself using your watch.

6. Turn over the next card. Do the matching exercise for 30 seconds. Repeat with the rest of the pack.

7. Aces are a special category. Each ace represents fast exercise. So when you turn over the ace of diamonds, you will do your 'diamonds exercise' for 30 seconds, but at an accelerated speed.

Don't fall into the trap of thinking that this is an easy workout: it is non-stop aerobic exercise for 26 minutes at a stretch. Do it several times a week, and your fitness levels will soar.

Strength to Strength walking and running programmes

If you are unused to regular exercise, these are good places to start. These programmes are effective, easy to follow and have been tailored to everyone. Once your routine is set, you will begin to see the results. You can also visit www.yourgoldenthreads.com for additional exercises and fitness ideas.

Follow the tables overleaf, choosing the age level that is right for you. Once you reach week 16, in order to sustain the cardio-vascular benefits achieved, simply continue with the programme as outlined in week 16.

Remember to spend five minutes stretching before running, and two minutes cooling down (this can include walking) after your run.

Strength to Strength walking programme
MEN AND WOMEN UNDER 40

Undertake this programme **three** times a week if you are combining it with a workout.

Undertake this programme **four to five** times a week if you are not combining it with a workout.

WEEK	DISTANCE	TIME
1	1.0 miles	16 minutes
2	1.0 miles	16 minutes
3	1.0 miles	15 minutes
4	1.0 miles	15 minutes
5	1.5 miles	23 minutes
6	1.5 miles	23 minutes
7	1.5 miles	22 minutes
8	1.5 miles	22 minutes
9	2.0 miles	32 minutes
10	2.0 miles	30 minutes
11	2.5 miles	38 minutes
12	2.5 miles	38 minutes
13	3.0 miles	48 minutes
14	3.0 miles	47 minutes
15	3.0 miles	45 minutes
16	3.0 miles	42 minutes

Strength to Strength running programme
MEN AND WOMEN UNDER 40

Undertake this programme **three** times a week if you are combining it with a workout.

Undertake this programme **four to five** times a week if you are not combing it with a workout.

WEEK	ACTIVITY	DISTANCE	TIME
1	Walk	1.0 miles	16 minutes
2	Walk	1.0 miles	16 minutes
3	Walk	1.0 miles	15 minutes
4	Walk	1.0 miles	15 minutes
5	Walk	1.5 miles	23 minutes
6	Walk	1.5 miles	23 minutes
7	Walk	1.5 miles	22 minutes
8	Walk	1.5 miles	22 minutes
9	Walk	2.0 miles	30 minutes
10	Walk	2.0 miles	30 minutes
11	Run	2.0 miles	26 minutes
12	Run	2.0 miles	24 minutes
13	Run	2.0 miles	22 minutes
14	Run	2.0 miles	20 minutes
15	Run	2.0 miles	19 minutes
16	Run	2.0 miles	17 minutes

Should you wish to increase your running distance to 3.0 miles after week 16, you should aim to do so in 28–30 minutes.

Strength to Strength walking programme

MEN AND WOMEN OVER 40

Undertake this programme **three** times a week if you are combining it with a workout.

Undertake this programme **four to five** times a week if you are not combining it with a workout.

WEEK	DISTANCE	TIME
1	1.0 miles	17 minutes
2	1.0 miles	17 minutes
3	1.0 miles	16 minutes
4	1.0 miles	16 minutes
5	1.5 miles	24 minutes
6	1.5 miles	24 minutes
7	1.5 miles	23 minutes
8	1.5 miles	23 minutes
9	2.0 miles	33 minutes
10	2.0 miles	32 minutes
11	2.5 miles	40 minutes
12	2.5 miles	40 minutes
13	3.0 miles	50 minutes
14	3.0 miles	48 minutes
15	3.0 miles	46 minutes
16	3.0 miles	45 minutes

Strength to Strength running programme
MEN AND WOMEN OVER 40

Undertake this programme **three** times a week if you are combining it with a workout.

Undertake this programme **four to five** times a week if you are not combining it with a workout.

WEEK	ACTIVITY	DISTANCE	TIME
1	Walk	1.0 miles	17 minutes
2	Walk	1.0 miles	17 minutes
3	Walk	1.0 miles	16 minutes
4	Walk	1.0 miles	16 minutes
5	Walk	1.5 miles	24 minutes
6	Walk	1.5 miles	24 minutes
7	Walk	1.5 miles	23 minutes
8	Walk	1.5 miles	23 minutes
9	Walk	2.0 miles	32 minutes
10	Walk	2.0 miles	31 minutes
11	Run	2.0 miles	28 minutes
12	Run	2.0 miles	26 minutes
13	Run	2.0 miles	25 minutes
14	Run	2.0 miles	24 minutes
15	Run	2.0 miles	22 minutes
16	Run	2.0 miles	20 minutes

How to get into a routine

It can be tough to get into the habit of exercising regularly, but it is always worthwhile. Here are 20 top tips that will help you to develop your routine – and to stick to it.

If you ever feel your resolve flagging, you may find it useful to come back and read these tips again.

1.　Give yourself a **compelling reason** for getting fit. It may be that you want to be able to play with your kids more, or that you want to decrease your risk of heart disease and other illnesses. Perhaps you hope that if you increase your energy levels, you can improve your performance at work. Once you have your compelling reason, stick with it.

2.　Getting started is the hardest part, but if you do something over and above what you are doing now – even if it's just walking the kids to school – you will discover the momentum and the mindset to move forward. The good feeling that you get after a workout or a walk will keep you going.

3.　There are plenty of **clubs and activities** from which to choose. If you opt for one that is linked to one of your interests or hobbies, you will find it easier to motivate yourself. If you like to dance, for example, perhaps you would enjoy a dance class. If you love the countryside, why not join a ramblers' club?

4.　You can build exercise into your life far more easily if you make a **regular time slot** for it every day. Write that time into your diary, and move the rest of your life around it.

5.　There is much debate about the **best time of day** for exercise. If you can, exercise before you begin work in the morning. It's the time of day when cares and concerns are at a minimum: it is too early for people from work to begin calling, and you will be feeling more refreshed and motivated than you do when you get home from work in the evening. If you have to, go to bed an hour earlier and get up an hour earlier.

6.   Pat yourself on the back. Praise and reward yourself when you set a new personal best, or when you succeed in sticking to your routine for a set period of time. Give yourself recognition for every step of progress that you make – even the baby steps.

7.   If you join a gym, **don't compare yourself to other people** there. Compare yourself with yourself: how you were when you joined, and how you are now.

8.   If you are a **first-timer** at the gym, let the staff know. They will show you around and explain how to use the various machines. There will also be personal trainers, who can take you around the gym on specially tailored workouts.

9.   If you are unsure about **how to use a particular machine** and there aren't any staff nearby, consult the diagrams on the wall or ask your fellow members. If you use a machine incorrectly, you could end up injuring yourself.

10. Don't dismiss **exercise DVDs**. If you like the style of a particular DVD and the exercises stretch you, keep on doing them.

11. Weigh yourself no more than once a week. If you step on the scales every day, you are doing yourself more harm than good. Hormonal cycles, eating habits and new exercise patterns mean that your body weight can vary by up to 4 pounds a day. If you jump on the scales and see your weight dipping up and down, you can become demoralised.

12. If **injury or illness** forces you to suspend your exercise routine, rest assured that there is always something you can do. Even if you are stuck in bed, you can still have a fitness regime. For example, you can increase your muscle power by isometric exercises (also known as static strength exercises), such as pressing the palms together in front of your body, holding the tension for 10 seconds and then relaxing and starting again.

Many of the exercises that feature in the playing card workout can be tailored to different injuries. It is a home-based workout and no additional equipment is required. Ask your GP or trainer for assistance.

13. Don't listen to any 'Fat Controllers' who poke fun at your new routine, or criticise you for spending time and money at the local gym. Why is it that the people who make a fuss about the cost of gym membership are often the ones who spend extortionate amounts of money on cigarettes, alcohol or other fripperies? The critics often prefer you to stay where you are, to make them feel better about their own mediocrity.

14. If you have someone around who will support you, let them know what you plan to achieve and **share your successes** with them. Exercise with a friend. If you are following a Strength to Strength walking programme, get other family members to come and walk with you. They will keep you motivated. The more support you can secure, the more likely you are to achieve your goal.

15. Work towards an event such as a walking weekend, a cycling holiday or a charity run. If you set yourself goals, you are likely to make a greater amount of progress in a shorter space of time.

16. If your preference is for **anaerobic exercise** such as weight training, that's fine. But be sure to take rests of no longer than

60 seconds between sets. Alternatively, supplement your fitness schedule with regular aerobic exercise such as running, swimming or cycling.

17. Buy a bicycle and cycle to work. Or buy an exercise bike and train at home. Be aware that a lot of home fitness equipment becomes towel rails and coat hangers, so install it only if you are committed to using it regularly.

18. Yoga and pilates can be less intensive than other workouts, but they are still valuable because they instil self-discipline and help you to focus on your body. They also increase stamina, suppleness and strength.

19. If you have an **mp3 player**, load it with your favourite tracks. When you take it to the gym or go running, you may find that losing yourself in your favourite music will help you to achieve more. (However, if you are tempted to take your mp3 player with you wherever you go, read the Spiritual Threads section.)

20. To **enjoy yourself** as much as possible while exercising, focus your mind upon the results, the benefits and the amazing feeling that you know you are going to have when your exercise session is over. Remind yourself over and over again why you are doing it, by viewing this picture of your happy, healthy self in your mind's eye.

SUMMARY

o When you are physically fit, you feel like a new you and your potential to achieve is greatly expanded. If you exercise regularly, you will be able to learn faster, think more clearly and remember more.

○   To improve your level of fitness, exercise or go to the gym at least three times a week. Ideally, exercise for 40 to 50 minutes in a session, and exercise up to six times per week.

○   The Strength to Strength playing card workout and the Strength to Strength walking and running programmes are suitable for beginners and experts alike and will help develop sound exercise routines.

○   Getting started is the hardest part, but there is much that you can do to keep yourself motivated.

ACTION POINTS

1. If you are taking up the Strength to Strength walking programme, map out your routes. You can do this using online maps, or by setting off in your car and keeping a careful eye on the odometer.

2. If you are in a position to make a financial investment in your future health, make an appointment for a 'health MOT'. In the UK there are some excellent centres dedicated to the provision of in-depth health checks, support and advice. We strongly recommend the Wellness Centre at adidas (UK) Ltd (www.wellnessinternational. co.uk): it provides full health and stress examinations together with 'lifestyle intervention programmes', which yield dramatic results. There is a Wellness Centre in Manchester, and one is also due to open in London.

3. If you do not have the right workout gear, get it. There isn't any need to spend large sums of money, but certain items are worthwhile investments. Proper running shoes and walking shoes, for example, will give improved results. A pack of cards, for the Strength to Strength playing card workout, costs next to nothing!

WORKSHEET

Look in the mirror and let it all hang out. What do you see: a god, or an *oh my god*? Look at the shape of your body, the texture of your skin, the brightness of your eyes and the condition of your hair. Do you look vital, alert and aware? Sometimes you don't need a thorough medical examination to know if you are healthy.

On a scale of 1 to 10 for health, where would you place yourself? Now where would you rather be? This is the starting point from which you will strengthen your Health Threads.

The following table is a Wellness Scale, which measures how good you feel. Fill out this table at the end of every week, starting this week. Enter a number between 1 and 10. If you are a 1, you are feeling sluggish, fatigued and low. If you are a 10, you are feeling energetic, motivated and healthy.

At the end of 10 weeks, look back over this table and observe how your sense of well-being has improved.

WEEK NUMBER	WELLNESS RATING (1–10)
1	
2	
3	
4	
5	
6	
7	
8	
9	
10	

PART

The Relationship Threads

CHAPTER 14

No man is an I-land

This section of the book is dedicated to improving your ability to form new relationships and keep existing ones in pristine condition. It also explores the positive, important roles that relationships of all kinds have to play in your life.

Why relationships are golden

Without love, human contact and a sense of belonging, what are you? What do you have?

If friendships or other relationships are notably lacking in your life, would you say that your life is balanced?

Human contact helps define us, because it influences our thoughts and actions. This is why babies can waste away and die if they are not touched, or if they have little contact with others. A century ago in America, when unwanted infants were deposited in large orphanages, it was reported that up to 99 per cent of them died within seven months. All their basic needs, except one, had been met. They were fed, cleaned, sheltered and clothed – but they lacked social contact.

In today's hospitals, sick or premature babies are sometimes treated with 'touch therapy'. They are touched, massaged or rocked at regular intervals throughout the day. Studies show that this treatment helps babies to get well sooner.

Babies aren't the only ones who benefit from this personal contact. A study has also shown that the hospital volunteers who rock or massage the infants have lower anxiety levels and improved self-esteem.

A recent scientific study used imaging techniques to show that when a person becomes socially excluded, changes take place inside the brain. The researchers also found that these changes in brain function can also affect other areas of a person's life, leading to poor decision-making, a reduced ability to learn and a lack of self-control.

Every one of us needs each of us. When communities are closer and richer, they are filled with emotional wealth.

66 You are uplifted when you have friends and supporters around you. 99

If you shut yourself away, you are missing out many times over.

That's what friends are for

After I suffered a significant setback with the loss of my health club business, my friends helped me and my family in so many ways. When we needed them, they were there. They comforted and supported us, and helped us to move onwards and upwards.

Two of our friends paid our mortgage for six months, and gave me an office to work from. Another couple stepped forward and insisted on paying our daughter's school fees; Emma was so happy at her school, and we knew that it would be very disruptive for her if she had to leave. Given the circumstances, we wanted her to be as settled as possible. On more than one occasion, the kindness shown by all of these friends reduced me to tears.

People said to me, 'You are so lucky to have such wonderful people in your life'. At that time I didn't see myself as lucky, but I will be forever grateful to my friends — not just because of what they did, but because of what their actions said about our relationships. Good friends such as these don't just appear out of the woodwork. The people with whom you surround yourself are the best possible indication of who you are and where you are in your own life.

Family relationships are inherited, and can be enriched with time and nurturing. Relationships outside the home are created from the ground up. They are of your own making. Friends, colleagues and acquaintances can all play different roles in your life, and you in theirs.

A true friend will provide emotional support or advice if you are challenged by a situation at home or at work. That friend will also feel comfortable calling upon you for support or advice. Acts of kindness – however small – and shared experiences leave you feeling good, and feed and strengthen your Golden Threads.

If you would like to develop good relationships at work, be a good colleague.

66 Conversation begins with not one, but three Cs: care, compassion and courage. 99

Monitor your own conversations on a daily basis. Become your own censor. Think on your feet. If you have a valid point to make, then make it without criticising, condemning or complaining. By replacing the three negative Cs in your conversation with their three positive counterparts, your ability to make and keep good relationships will improve dramatically.

If you spend more time listening than conversing, or if somebody is using you as their personal sounding board, it may be time to review that relationship. Good, productive relationships are two-way streets: you add value to one another's lives.

Your relationships define you

Look around and take stock of your friends and acquaintances.

What are they like? Do they condemn, criticise and complain? Are they honest? What are their interests? What do they say? Do you enjoy listening to them? Are they generous with their time and attention? Are you comfortable around them? When you can answer in the affirmative, you are on the right track. If you can't, isn't it time to upgrade the circles in which you move?

One-way relationships, which are not founded on mutual respect, admiration and interest, add little value to your Golden Rope.

When I started to rebuild my lifestyle, giving away my businesses and deciding to make a fresh start, I quickly discovered that I didn't have many friends. My phone stopped ringing. Nobody came round to see me. It was if I had fallen off a cliff.

This was a valuable learning experience, but I will admit that it was also a painful one. Before, I had been a big fish in a little pond. My friends were bodybuilders, debt collectors and doormen. But when I wasn't useful to them anymore, they didn't want to know me. They wanted to stay where they were, in their crowded comfort zone. When I leapt out of the pond, I was on my own.

Looking back, it was for the best. Bradford wasn't a pleasant place at the time, and my then-friends were rooted into a self-seeking culture of drink, drugs and crime – a lifestyle I was determined to leave behind. They weren't bad people, but I no longer wanted to be one of them and I no longer wanted that kind of life. They prided themselves on their designer clothes and 'tough' reputations. I wanted to get away from all that.

And now I am so thankful that our lives parted and I took a different path. Sadly for my old associates, life soon spiralled downwards. A former colleague of mine got hooked on crack cocaine and became a prostitute, and one of my oldest school friends fled overseas after his life was threatened by a local gang. Another was convicted of armed robbery.

These relationships were flimsy threads, brittle and easily broken. They weren't Golden Threads. I put them to one side, and began building my Relationship Threads from scratch.

SUMMARY

⦿   All the relationships in your life are Golden Threads, which add value to your life and the lives of others.

⦿   The people in your life help define you, by influencing your thoughts and actions.

⦿   Every one of us needs each of us. If you shut yourself off from those around you, you are missing out.

⦿   One-way relationships, which are not founded on mutual respect and admiration, should be reconsidered.

ACTION POINTS

1.   Run through your friends and associates, one by one, in your mind. For each person, ask yourself these questions: is this person a friend, an associate, or an acquaintance? If your life took a turn for the worse, would they still be there for you? If their life took a turn for the worse, would you be there for them? By being very clear about what your relationships mean to you, you can avoid unrealistic expectations and disappointment.

2.   If you were in trouble or confused, to whom would you turn for advice and support? A variety of circumstances require a variety of qualities and skills. Here are three sample scenarios:

a. You are having a difficult time at work.

b. Your relationship with your partner becomes bumpy.

c. You receive some wonderful personal news, and you would like to celebrate.

For each of these scenarios ask yourself, who would you call? If more than one person comes to mind for each one, you have a good foundation upon which to build other productive relationships.

3. Get out your diary. When will you be free over the next couple of weeks? Pick up the phone and plan to meet a friend whom you haven't seen for months or years.

WORKSHEET

Following the example below, in the table overleaf list six relationships in your life and describe how your life has benefited from each of them. The list should feature a mix of family members, friends, work colleagues and other relationships. The benefits to your life can be material (such as a gift or a loan), non-material (emotional support in a time of need, for example) or a mixture of both.

Example

Name: Sue   Relationship: Neighbour

Benefit: Keeping an eye on the house when we are away, to give us peace of mind. Babysitting when we had a family emergency

Name : _____   Relationship: _____

Benefit:

_____

Name : _____   Relationship: _____

Benefit:

_____

Name : _____   Relationship: _____

Benefit:

_____

Name : _____   Relationship: _____

Benefit:

_____

Name : _____   Relationship: _____

Benefit:

_____

Name : _____   Relationship: _____

Benefit:

_____

From this list, choose one of the people described and write a short note to them. Tell them why you value them so highly, and thank them for being there for you. Even if you feel shy about doing this, go ahead: it will be a rewarding experience for both of you.

CHAPTER 15

Tend to your friends

Relationships are like roses: getting them to bud is the hardest part. Once they begin to bloom, however, you must continue to cultivate them. If neglected, they wither and die on the stem.

Sometimes we can be so immersed within our day-to-day lives, or so focused upon forging exciting new friendships and alliances, we forget to give due care and attention to our existing relationships. Before we know it, those relationships have fizzled away.

It doesn't help that we now spend so much of our time on the internet and on our mobile phones. In theory e-mail, text messaging services and social networking websites such as Facebook and Twitter should make it easier for us to keep in touch with people. However, they can't beat a relaxing evening with friends, a meal with a few people, a barbecue with neighbours, an evening of cards or an outdoor team game.

Relationships are constantly evolving; for example, you may develop an enduring friendship with a work colleague that, over a period of time, grows beyond the workplace.

66 To get the most out of any relationship, keep contributing to it. 99

Six simple ways to strengthen relationships

1. Be sincere. When you make positive comments, always be earnest and truthful. If you are insincere, it usually shows; dishonesty breeds distrust, and you will be suspected of having a game plan. If people know that you are trustworthy and will give them straight answers, they will come to you for advice when they are in difficult situations.

2. Don't talk about people behind their backs. The only thing that you should do behind a person's back is pat it. If you talk about a person who isn't there, don't say anything that would make you uncomfortable if you said it to their face. Loyalty is an attractive quality, and is central to every enduring relationship.

3. Show that you value your relationships. Take an interest in other people's families, work and plans. If you make them feel great about themselves, they will enjoy spending time with you – and vice versa.

Awaken or reawaken relationships by spending time together. Go for occasional weekends away; go running or walking together; go to away matches, to see your favourite football teams play.

4. Be generous with your time. Life is hectic and your time is a prized commodity. It is an investment: lavish it upon relationships that are important to you, and you will receive dividends in return.

66 If every second was a pound coin, how would your time be spent? 99

A good friend of mine worked hard to establish his business. From nothing he created a successful enterprise worth £8 million with 220 staff over 42 sites. Quite an achievement in anyone's eyes.

Inevitably he reached the point where he realised he had taken the company as far as he could and he faced the prospect of selling it. A hard thing to do when you have invested so much of yourself into a business and I knew it would be a difficult time for him.

As his friend, I wanted to help him through the process. We spent a lot of time together discussing the sale. I helped him look at the situation with a fresh pair of eyes, so that he could see the benefits of leaving behind the long hours, high levels of personal risk and how he would enjoy spending more time on himself and his life outside work.

I hope he found my advice useful, but more importantly he knew I was there for him as a 'mate'.

5. Be there when the going gets tough. Sometimes when people are experiencing difficulties they just want a sympathetic ear. Often, if you can spend time with them and listen, they will come up with their own answers. Your presence and support are what count: you are there when they need you, and you never let them down.

6. Refuse to let valuable relationships fall off the radar. Make an occasional habit of leafing through your address book, or scrolling through your mobile phone's contacts list. Whenever you spot the name of anyone to whom you haven't spoken in the past few months, give them a quick call and catch up with them.

If they are pleased to hear from you – and they usually are – there should be plenty to talk about and you can pick that Golden Thread up again. Your next step, if appropriate, is to arrange to see them.

Mentors

Mentors may be found in work environments, social environments or places in which you would never have expected to find them.

What all mentors have in common is that they represent some of the strongest Relationship Threads. They help you to improve yourself in a particular area of your life, giving you aspirations, inspirations and fresh confidence. They share knowledge and initiate shortcuts to success, by steering you away from pitfalls. The chances are that, wherever you are in your life, someone has been there before you. As previously noted, such a person is the perfect mentor, because they are living proof that your ambitions can be achieved.

You may be in a position to mentor someone else. There is a lot of spiritual satisfaction to be gained from holding out your hand to someone and passing on your passion. Mentoring also compels you to improve yourself, by plunging you into regular contact with someone who takes a deep interest in your achievements and abilities. When somebody looks up to you, you want to fulfil their expectations; often you go the extra mile to make sure that you do. A deep connection between the two of you will ensure that you both enjoy the journey.

One of my mentors was Bob Sweeney. We met when we were both spectators at a bodybuilding contest in the late 1970s. As it happened, we were in the same business: I had one health club at that time, and Bob had four. He was older than me and ahead of me when it came to the management of successful fitness centres. He made frequent overseas business trips and was a member of the Association of Physical Fitness Centers in America.

I really liked him as a person. His energy and enthusiasm for health and fitness were infectious. He was able to run his business from a distance, which was a quality I greatly admired and hoped to replicate. It was a feat that required accurate management systems and processes, and Bob had an eagle eye for figures. He was dynamic, focused and ahead of the game at that time. We clicked, and I was keen to learn as much from him as I could.

I managed to secure Bob as a mentor when I persuaded him to go into partnership with me. We opened our first joint fitness centre in Sheffield. We drew up the plans together; I managed the building project and once the club was in operation we split the profits. We went on to open two more clubs together, one in Keighley and one in Wakefield. I travelled to America with him; we attended annual conventions of health club owners, purchased state-of-the-art equipment, made many interesting new business contacts and returned with many profitable marketing strategies.

He was a willing mentor and we continued to get on well with one another. We both gained much from this relationship: while Bob was helping me to grow as a businessman, I was growing our business. The clubs became hugely successful. Much of what I learned from him – such as how to produce accurate analyses of membership income, and how to put key performance indicators in place – I still use today.

Bob came into my life at a perfect time. All these years later, we remain friends.

SUMMARY

◉ To get the most out of any relationship, you have to keep working at it. The more you put in, the more you will get back.

◉ You can do much to maintain and strengthen existing relationships.

◉ Mentors are valuable because they can help clear your path to long-term success. They encourage you to improve yourself and make the most of your abilities. Their advice is borne of personal experience, and they are living proof of what can be achieved in your chosen field.

ACTION POINTS

1. Go into a bookshop, or visit the online bookstore at www. yourgoldenthreads.com. Find a book that you think a friend or associate would enjoy. Send it to them, along with a personal note. You can guarantee that they will be pleased to receive a surprise gift.

2. If you don't have a mentor, make a list of the qualities that your ideal mentor would possess. What would they have experienced, and what would they have achieved? Your list may help you to identify a would-be mentor with whom you already have a personal or professional relationship. At the very least, this exercise will help to identify your mentor when he or she does come into your life.

While you are looking for your real-life mentor, you can also visit sites such as www.horsesmouth.co.uk, for free mentoring online.

3. Organise an event for a group of people with whom you have a good personal or professional relationship. This could be a weekend away together, a private tour of a stately home or lunch in a popular new restaurant. Pick an event that people will remember as having been special.

WORKSHEET
In the table overleaf, follow the example below and enter the names of six people with whom you have relationships. You could pick your partner or children, in-laws, work colleagues, friends or social acquaintances. For each relationship, mark yourself out of 10 for the effort that you put into maintaining it, and write down one thing that you could do to cement or improve that relationship.

Give yourself one month to put your suggestions into effect, then rescore yourself.

Example

Name: David Brown   Relationship: Work Colleague   Score: 6

Action: Offer to take him to lunch   Rescore: 7

Name: Relationship: Score:

Action: Rescore:

Name: Relationship: Score:

Action: Rescore:

Name: Relationship: Score:

Action: Rescore:

Name: Relationship: Score:

Action: Rescore:

Name: Relationship: Score:

Action: Rescore:

Name: Relationship: Score:

Action: Rescore:

CHAPTER 16

New faces

I f you are to create a strong network of Relationship Threads for your Golden Rope, it is essential that you build upon the relationships you already have. However, it is also important to introduce new faces into your life.

66 An ability to forge fresh relationships is key to your future success. 99

New people often lead to new opportunities. This principle holds true no matter who you are, where you are in your life or what your ambitions for the future may be. When you step outside your comfort zone, or beyond the limits of your current social circle, you will discover that one person, one event, one new comment or one new idea can be all it takes to shift your life into a higher gear and a new direction. If you stay where you are, you could miss out on an opportunity that would lead you to a new and exciting future.

Your chances of success and achievement are greatly improved when you meet strangers and get to know new acquaintances. For example:

○ **Paul Newman** launched his extremely successful food product range, 'Newman's Own', after meeting his Connecticut neighbour, the writer A.E. Hotchner, and going into partnership with him. 'The friendship was the whole key', Hotchner once said, when explaining how the two men spurred one another on. 'It never would have happened without it.'

○ Award-winning guitar-maker **Jim Fleeting** found out about the guitar-making school in Arizona from the American bass builder Ken Smith, after he introduced himself to Ken and asked for job advice. Jim won a place to study at the prestigious school, left his old job in the City and embarked upon his dream career.

o   The actress **Julie Walters**'s career took off after she met the comedienne and writer Victoria Wood at the Bush Theatre in London, in 1978. After the pair appeared together in a television series called *Wood and Walters*, Julie Walters shot to fame in the film *Educating Rita* and has since appeared in a number of roles created for her by her good friend Wood, most notably, 'Mrs Overall' in the spoof soap opera, *Acorn Antiques*.

Right now you may be thinking that because you put so much effort into keeping your current relationships in good order, you don't have the time or the inclination to seek additional relationships elsewhere. Or you may be perfectly happy with your current social circle. If you would rather stay where you are, you should do so.

However, it is worth bearing in mind that inspiration and good ideas often come from the most unexpected sources and situations. By enriching your life with new relationships of many kinds, you are investing in your own future.

How to create new relationships

Many people get nervous about meeting strangers. Some people can become settled or inflexible in their ways; others, when immersed in unfamiliar circumstances or situations, are inclined to keep themselves to themselves and shut themselves off from what they do not know. Many of us are spending increasing amounts of time online, playing virtual games or cultivating virtual contacts and acquaintances. Some of us are challenged by the idea of turning our focus away from those small, bright computer screens and towards real people in real worlds.

Once you begin meeting new people, however, nerves are soon forgotten. When you step outside your front door, you will discover that new Relationship Threads are simple and straightforward to create.

- Begin by identifying a **particular area of your life** that you hope to improve, or a subject in which you hold an interest. For example, you may wish to start your own business, or you could have a long-held ambition to learn a foreign language.

- Draw upon your **Six Honest Serving Men** to fill your mind with 'whats' and 'whys'. *Why* should I go there to meet people? *Why* do I need to? *What* will I gain? Find answers to these questions. For example: if you intend to join a gym club so that you can lose weight, identify *why* you desire to do this. Perhaps you don't wish to be overweight because you want to get involved in your children's sporting activities. Perhaps you hope to live longer, by reducing your risk factors for conditions such as heart disease and type 2 diabetes. The better you understand your motivations, the stronger those motivations will become.

- Find out about **local organisations**, clubs, groups and places in your locality that offer opportunities in your chosen area. If you have business ambitions, you could begin with your local chamber of commerce, where you will find like-minded individuals and a shared interest in building successful companies. If you wish to learn a foreign language, find out about classes offered at evening schools and adult education centres. You can find lists and links to national and regional education centres and membership organisations at the Golden Threads website: www.yourgoldenthreads.com

- If you can, **find a friend** to accompany you to the first event. If they already belong to your chosen group, all the better: they will be able to furnish you with valuable introductions.

- To access a **database** of people in your local area, who have read this book and share your interests, sign up to the *Strength* *to Strength Group* section of www.yourgoldenthreads.com. This resource can help you find like-minded people with whom to attend groups and events.

- **Get moving**. If you can't find anyone to go with you, despite your best efforts, don't use this as a reason for waiting. Don't wait until the end of the month, or the beginning of next year. Just go. Think about it: if your chosen event or group turns out to be wrong for you, what have you lost? Nothing more than a few hours of your time.

- When you meet people for the first time, take care to **avoid hasty judgements**. First impressions can be off the mark. If you follow your instincts, prepare to be mistaken on occasion.

- At the same time, remember to **keep your eye on the future**. Search out those individuals who remind you of what you want to be, do and have. If no one is on hand to introduce you, jump in with both feet and introduce yourself. Seize the initiative and begin asking questions. Do more listening than talking; you will learn so much more.

- The stronger your other Golden Threads, the better. **Like attracts like**. If you are happy and full of energy, you will draw other energised, happy people towards you.

❝ Dynamic, friendly people tend to have friendly, dynamic friends. ❞

- If you admire somebody and hope to know them better, it is easier to **find common ground** if you already share some of their qualities.

When I left my old life behind, my determination to carve a new future for myself led me to many places, people and meetings. I began adding new Golden Threads to a very tattered rope, one at a time.

I found that my efforts had a domino effect: one meeting led to another and before I knew it, I was surrounded by new people and opportunities. Just one year after cutting my old threads and ties, I found myself in Florida, speaking at business seminars and spending time with new friends.

So what did I do? I kept my eyes and ears open. I began saying 'yes' to people, and didn't shy from sticking my toes into unchartered waters. One of my first positive actions was to meet up with Barry again, having not seen him in years. He spoke highly of a smart new health club that had opened in my area, so I went and signed up. The club had a busy social calendar, with regular barbecues and other events. I went to as many of these events as I could, and soon came to know others who shared my interests. One man was a squash fanatic, and he invited me to his squash club. When I accompanied him, he introduced me to his circle there: ambitious, middle-class businesspeople, who were very different to my previous associates.

At around the same time I became involved with a network-marketing organisation, with the aim of kick-starting my career. I soon found that I had become part of a small community of instant mentors and people who shared my desire for self-improvement. Their drive was contagious.

There, I met someone who told me about Toastmasters, a global public-speaking organisation. I joined a local branch to improve my presentation skills, and went on to make a number of valuable contacts.

Someone else recommended seminars hosted by a personal development publisher. These turned out to be great places for meeting like-minded men and women. After one of these seminars, I began talking to a man named Paul Greaves. He knew a lot about telecommunications: an industry about which, at that time, I knew little. His tips, advice and ideas encouraged me to found my first telecommunications company. We still enjoy a good working relationship.

Before long, I had a new group of friends. Instead of spending my spare time in pubs or clubs with people who were filling their glasses and emptying their heads, I was going for dinner with new acquaintances in Humberside, or driving down to the Midlands, south coast or Edinburgh for weekend breaks at friends' homes. These people liked to use their heads, and these new relationships stimulated and inspired me. We found common ground in our interests, and often talked about our plans and ideas long into the night. The evenings were a world away from what I had previously known.

These Relationships Threads have made my Golden Rope much stronger. I have heard it said that, as you get older, it becomes more difficult to meet new people. My experience has been the opposite.

Fighting the fear factors

For various reasons, many people feel uncomfortable about going to unfamiliar places and surrounding themselves with strangers. Some fear rejection or discomfort if they step out of their comfort zones. Others lack self-esteem, or convince themselves that they cannot afford to go out, or that they will not fit in. These are the most common barriers to new relationships – but with a little courage, they can all be overcome.

- **Shyness**. This isn't a disease, or an irreversible affliction. You aren't born with it. However, a reluctance to meet and greet new people has obvious drawbacks.

   Jump in at the deep end: you will find that you can swim. If you suffer from shyness, confront it. Meet it head on; the initial challenges will be outweighed by the benefits. If you find this too uncomfortable, choose an alternative plan of action that will help you to overcome your shyness and meet new people, such as hypnotherapy or group volunteer work.

- **Low self-esteem**. If you have a poor vision or opinion of yourself, you are likely to gravitate towards others who suffer from this state of mind. You may talk yourself out of opportunities, because you don't believe that you are worthy of them. You may be tempted to ease your nerves with medication – a bad idea, for many reasons. There are no quick fixes for this problem, but if you put as much effort as you can into improving yourself by building strong Golden Threads in all areas of your life – Spiritual Threads in particular – you will find that your self-esteem is gradually transformed for the better.

- **Lack of money**. This is a frequent, but inadequate excuse. You may have to look harder to find opportunities that will expand your social circle without emptying your wallet, but rest assured that they are there. Clubs run by volunteers from your community often cost next to nothing.

My wife and I co-founded a successful frozen food company with two of our friends. Our products are sold in supermarkets and shops around the country. However, the company would not have gone on to enjoy the good fortune that it has if we had not put a great deal of time and effort into going to new places, meeting new people and getting to know individuals who have gone on to play instrumental roles in the company's fortunes.

One example that stands out was when we joined a group of specialist food producers called Yorkshire Pantry. We had started our company and built a factory and a product range but, being new to the food industry, we needed somebody senior with in-depth industry knowledge and contacts who could run our business.

The very first event that we attended was the organisation's AGM, with drinks and dinner. We were very excited about going, even though we knew nobody there. Once we arrived, we began talking to people and explaining who we were. At the bar, I introduced myself to a man named Dennis Simpson. I couldn't know it then, but this was the beginning of a new, extremely important relationship for our company. The two of us continued talking over dinner and I began to realise that he could be an asset to our business.

Just weeks later, Dennis left his job heading a food company in Leeds – and we were able to snap him up, initially on a part-time basis. Before long, he was our new MD. With his help, our business has gone from strength to strength. That one night has led to many other contacts and many new Golden Threads. I am certainly glad that we made the effort. The experience has confirmed my belief that when it comes to venturing into the unknown and forging new relationships, you shouldn't hold yourself back. Just jump in with both feet, and do all that you can to begin building new relationships with new people. Had I not jumped in and met Dennis that night, I can't imagine how our company would have fared.

SUMMARY

○ By enriching your life with new relationships of many kinds, you are investing in your future. New people lead to new ideas and opportunities, no matter who you are, where you are in your life or what your ambitions are.

○ Seek out those individuals who exemplify what you want to be, do and have.

○ Like attracts like. If you admire somebody and hope to get to know them better, it's easier to find common ground if you already share some of their qualities.

○ Don't allow fears of rejection and ridicule to hold you back. Most barriers to new relationships can be knocked down.

ACTION POINTS

1. Join at least one new members' organisation in the next week. It could be anything from a night class to the Women's Institute or your local Chamber of Commerce, but choose the organisation that best fits your life's needs at this time.

2. Always carry business cards with you, or cards that list your contact details. Keep some handy in your pocket, or your bag. Sprinkle them like confetti over the people that you meet.

3. If you don't yet have a mentor, but you know a person who would be perfect for the role, have the courage to call them and invite them out for a coffee or for lunch. Have a list of questions ready. Explain what it is that you most admire about them and tell them why you wanted to meet up with them. It could be the best lunchtime investment that you ever make.

WORKSHEET

It can be surprisingly quick and easy to form new relationships. In the table below, provide details of the first five new relationships that you begin to build after reading this chapter, following the printed example. They should all be relationships for which you have high hopes. You don't have to complete this worksheet immediately, but if you add your new friends and associates one by one you will find that, before long, the table is full.

Example

Name: **Sara Smith**   Organisation : **Institute of Directors**

Background:

Met at breakfast event for new members. She owns a business similar size to mine. We are from different industries but face similar challenges

Your hopes for this relationship

That we can use one another as a sounding board for advice and ideas

Name: Organisation :

Background:

Your hopes for this relationship

Name: _____ Organisation : _____

Background:

_____

Your hopes for this relationship

_____

Name: _____ Organisation : _____

Background:

_____

Your hopes for this relationship

_____

Name: _____ Organisation : _____

Background:

_____

Your hopes for this relationship

_____

Name: _____ Organisation : _____

Background:

_____

Your hopes for this relationship

_____

PART

7

The Family Threads

CHAPTER 17

Family fortune

Your Family Threads are a valuable part of your Golden Rope. This is because your family keeps you grounded in success, keeps you motivated and keeps you focused when times are tough. You all share and enjoy one another's lives. You are all on a journey together. When you want to cry, your family builds you back up and makes you smile again.

Employers looking for salespeople often make beelines for candidates with young families. Why? Because these employees tend to be ambitious and highly motivated. They have families who support them – and who require support in return. These workers won't walk out if they have a bad day.

The journalist Erma Bombeck described her own family very neatly. She wrote, 'We were a strange little band of characters trudging through life sharing diseases and toothpaste, coveting one another's desserts, hiding shampoo, borrowing money, locking each other out of our rooms, inflicting pain and kissing to heal it in the same instant, loving, laughing, defending, and trying to figure out the common thread that bound us all together.'

Their 'common thread', of course, was love. Likewise, every member of your family represents a Golden Thread in your life.

Together, you make one another stronger.

After my nervous breakdown, I don't know how I could have put my troubles behind me without my family's support. Their concerns, thoughtfulness and confidence in me made all the difference. My five brothers and sisters all had kind, sympathetic words and helped me to claw back some of my self-esteem. My mother lavished care and attention on me; she made delicious stews, pancakes and homemade soups, which she made with love. Their support certainly helped to speed up my recovery.

Decades later, I went through another tough time when my health club business folded – and my family came around me, just as before.

This experience of losing my business brought home to me what it was that I cherished most. My wife and children are the most important people in my life, and the love and support that we gave one another helped us all to get through the difficulties that followed. My wife Janet was upset to lose our beautiful home, but she was determined to look towards our future. She was – and is – an amazing person.

The years I had spent creating my Golden Rope meant that I was able to stay strong and make a successful comeback, but it is impossible for me to imagine my life without my family. We aren't The Waltons: we all have our highs and lows. But when any member of my family experiences a challenging or turbulent period in life, they can count upon the rest of us to come around them in the same way that the family gathered to support me when I needed them most. This is what matters. I don't think I would have had the same amount of motivation if I hadn't been in a position to draw strength and support from my loved ones.

Families at war

Families aren't perfect. All too often, terrible rifts result from the smallest of events or disagreements. A few throwaway words or a misjudged decision can spark a row that escalates into a full-blown estrangement, with relationships permanently damaged or destroyed.

The solution? 'Tinker tacks'. Hundreds of years ago, tinkers used to travel from town to town, fixing broken pots, lids and china with the tiniest of nails. This work required a lot of skill and care: a tinker-tacked lid, for example, would look as good as new. It was only when you turned it over that you would see the tell-tale line of tacks that held that lid together.

Family relationships are like crockery. They can be fragile and they can shatter. However, if you are willing to put in the necessary time and effort, just as the tinkers did when they mended valuable household goods, most relationships can be repaired. If you leave your family relationships in their broken state, set to one side, that is where they will stay.

Single and child-free?

If you are happy on your own, don't feel pressured into changing. But note that 'family' doesn't begin and end with spouses and children. Your family may include parents, grandparents, uncles, aunts, nieces, nephews and other relatives. Do make the effort to stay in close contact with members of your extended family: if contact drops off, the relationship will probably fall away too.

If you don't have any family members to speak of, or if you are actively searching for someone with whom to spend your life, remember that life is a mirror. What you give out is what you get back. Get out there and mix with people. Enjoy the time that you spend with others as much as you can.

Work–life balance

When you are driven to succeed in your professional life, it becomes easy to neglect the people around you. However, when you imagine yourself in the future, looking back on your life – what we call 'Rocking Chair Thinking' – what will you see and how will you feel? Will you feel warm and uplifted when you recall all those hours that you put in at the office? When you think about all those promotions you sought and all that time you spent at the computer, will you have a tear in your eye?

It's unlikely, isn't it?

You are a human *being* – not a human *doing*. We are here to be, not to do. Life is about *feelings* as much as it is about actions. Sometimes you will have to burn the midnight oil to get things done, but always make sure that you enjoy some playtime before you move on to your next work project. Do whatever it takes to ensure that you and your family come first in one another's lives.

 Children spell love 'T-I-M-E'.

Strengthening your Family Threads

It is easy to tell when your Family Threads are strong. Family members may squabble occasionally, but they look one another in the eyes. When you look around you, what you see and feel is joy. If you have children, they are willing to open up to you. Even when you ask sensitive questions, they will answer honestly.

For robust Family Threads, follow these pointers:

1. Eat together. There is truth in the saying that 'the family that eats together, stays together'. Evidence suggests that children gain as much from family mealtimes as the adults do: a 1999 study found that when children were asked what they thought they would remember best about that period in their lives, they chose mealtimes over 'special events' such as holidays. A 1998 study concluded that children who ate with their parents five times a week were less likely to become depressed or to take drugs as children who ate with their parents three times a week. They were better at forming friendships with other children and were more motivated at school. Sadly, busy modern lives have meant that on average, today's children spend 12 fewer hours with their parents every week than children did two decades ago.

When you eat and relax as a family, talking and listening to one another on a daily basis, your Family Threads can only become stronger. You become more connected to one another. Any problems or conflicts are flagged up sooner, rather than later.

So don't allow your children to carry their plates up to their rooms. If you don't have a dining table, get one. Live your lives together, rather than separately.

2. Let your family know you love them. Tell them on a regular basis. They will respond in kind. When your loved ones put their arms around you and tell you that they love you too, it feels wonderful. It gives you a reason for being. Everyone responds to praise, so give it as often as you can. It means a lot to us, especially when we are young and struggling to find what we are good at. Not every child can shine in the classroom but if you can identify your child's gifts, you can help develop them. David Beckham wasn't particularly academic – but somebody spotted his footballing potential!

3. Go for family walks. These don't have to cost you a single penny, are always enjoyable and will bring your family together. Walk with your parents, your children or other members of your family. Take a picnic, or stop for ice cream. Spend time together out in the countryside, sitting by rivers or exploring landmarks and areas of natural beauty. Let the children run around and be themselves. Make the most of the fresh air. Search together for flowers or for flat stones to throw at the water. Take pleasure in one another's company.

4. When you plan a family holiday, plan it together. Ask everyone for their ideas and combine them to create a holiday that has everyone excited. Where will you go? What will you do when you are there? The teamwork and the shared enthusiasm will bring you together and ensure that everybody gets the most out of the family experience.

I am blessed with strong Family Threads: two wonderful sons and a wife who stands next to me in everything that I do.

I met Jo 15 years ago, at a course to improve public speaking skills, and I knew immediately that she was The One. Unfortunately I had no money at the time. I had to borrow my mum's car – a little white Nissan with a pink go-faster stripe – when I wanted to go somewhere. Expensive days or nights out were not an option, but Jo didn't mind. Instead we enjoyed one another's company so much that my finances, or lack thereof, were largely irrelevant. We visited friends and family, swam together and went for long walks and runs in the countryside.

With Jo's support and assistance, I founded my first company. When my telecommunications company first became successful, she turned her back on her own flourishing career and came to work in our fledgling family business, liaising with customers and chasing creditors. Her efforts were key to the company's transformation into a slick, professional enterprise.

Without her, would I be where I am now? Probably not. My family's unwavering enthusiasm, support and confidence in me has pushed me to do my best and has helped me to realise my potential.

SUMMARY

- Your Family Threads are valuable because your family motivates you, supports you and keeps you focused when times are tough.

- Don't let small squabbles or incidents escalate, hamper or damage your family life. Never go to sleep on an argument.

- Don't let your family take second place to your work; they have a prominent role to play in your happiness.

○ To strengthen your Family Threads, spend as much time as you can relaxing as a family. Talk, listen and gain maximum value from one another's company.

ACTION POINTS

1. If you are with any family members right now, put this book down for a minute. Go and tell them that you love and appreciate them. Do it now! If they are not with you at the moment, write notes to them.

2. Over the coming week, do one small favour for your partner every day, to show how much you value him or her. This could be running a hot bath for them when they are due home, valeting their car or cooking a surprise meal. If your partner begins doing the same for you, you may wish to continue this new tradition.

3. If you have fallen out with a family member in the past and it is some time since you made contact with them, give them a call or write them a short note.

WORKSHEET

In the table opposite write the names of family members and your relationship to them. Then describe what it is about them that you love the most.

When you have completed the table, take five postcards. Write out these bullet points, address the cards to the relevant members of your family, and distribute them.

Example

Name: Jane

Relationship: Mother

What I love:

- The knowledge that she will be always be here for me.
- When she telephones me, because she can tell when something is wrong.
- Her generosity and willingness to lend a hand.
- Her unfailing ability to see the bright side of every situation.

Name:

Relationship:

What I love:

-
-
-
-

Name:

Relationship:

What I love:

-
-
-
-

Name:

Relationship:

What I love:

-

-

-

-

Name:

Relationship:

What I love:

-

-

-

-

Name:

Relationship:

What I love:

-

-

-

-

PART

The Spiritual Threads

CHAPTER 18

Food for the
soul

Mind, body and spirit tend to be lumped together. The first two are straightforward; the third, less so. The words 'spirit' and 'spiritual' tend to conjure images of supplicants in prayer, or people in kaftans waving dream catchers around.

The spirit is a challenging concept because it isn't tangible. You can't see or touch it, but it's always there. Whatever it is, it's very private. Often, if you ask people about their beliefs, faith or personal philosophy, you can tell from their body language or stony silences that they are uncomfortable.

It's a no-go area for some – but we are going there anyway.

Many people avoid mention of the spiritual, because they don't want to impose or intrude upon other people's private beliefs – or lack of them – in any way. This is an understandable decision.

However your spirit, or your sense of self, is key to the way you live your life – regardless of what you think or believe.

66 Self worth is everything. Without it, life is a misery. 99 (Julie Walters)

Your sense of self is at the centre of all that you are and all that you do. It is the pivot upon which your life turns. If that pivot becomes weak, or askew, your Golden Rope will unravel around it.

This is probably the most challenging section of the book, but arguably the most important. Throughout your life there will often be times when you need to draw upon your inner strength. This section shows you how, by strengthening your Spiritual Threads, you can find happiness and fulfilment in hitherto hidden places.

What are the Spiritual Threads?

Their abstract nature makes them difficult to define, but let's put this question another way. When your Learning Threads are strong, the proof is in the action: you are always on the move, taking in new experiences and striving to meet new challenges. When your Health Threads are strong, people can tell by looking at you: you have a healthy body shape, your eyes sparkle, your complexion is clear and you have boundless energy. But when your Spiritual Threads are strong, how can you tell?

In many ways, Spiritual Threads resemble Learning Threads. All these threads represent a journey of the mind and an expansion of possibilities, and are based upon continuous progress.

However, they are not the same. Learning Threads are built around specific needs in your life, with various ends in mind. Strong Learning Threads enable you to set new bests and mark new milestones, such as career ambitions or personal triumphs. Learning Threads are goal-oriented. Spiritual Threads are not. Spiritual Threads are built around the sense of self: that inner identity that is physically undetectable, always present and in a state of continual change and development.

Strong Spiritual Threads are most easily defined by their tangible benefits and results. These apply regardless of faith, belief system or philosophy, and can be described as follows:

- An ability to be at peace with yourself. A sense of inner calm.
- An ability to live in the moment.
- An enjoyment of your everyday life with your family and friends.
- An ability to step outside of yourself and see the 'bigger picture'.
- An ability to detect when people are hurting or are facing personal challenges, and the ability to comfort them.
- A keen sense of responsibility for others.
- An ability to catch what life throws at you.

Why your Spiritual Threads are valuable

There is a common idea that 'what goes around, comes around': what you give out is what you can expect to receive in return. If you view yourself in negative terms, you cannot but view others negatively. By the same token, if you are a positive and contented person, who goes out of your way to help yourself and others, you will find that others are prepared to go the extra mile for you, too. The benefits can be immense.

❝ Your Spiritual Threads keep you in balance with other people and relationships. ❞

Spiritual Threads shrink the conflict in your life, by strengthening a sense of purpose in tandem with a positive, productive outlook.

Strong Spiritual Threads give you the comfort of knowing that you can stay in control and overcome whatever life throws at you.

I once had business dealings with a man who had all the trappings of success. He had beautiful homes in three of the UK's most expensive places to live. He had a brash attitude, a young trophy wife, a Ferrari and a yacht moored at Monte Carlo. 'Where did it all go wrong?' I joked with him.

Later I discovered that all was not what it seemed. This man's debts and creditors were mounting – and he owed me more than £1 million from a failed business transaction – yet he continued to spend money like water. When he lost everything, he did so quite literally: he was left with nothing, and nowhere to go. His identity had been more than 'crushed' – it was as if it had been erased. His sense of self was limited to material possessions. Once these material possessions were peeled away, there wasn't anything left.

Even though this man owed me money, I tried to help him as best I could, visiting banks with him and liaising with the receivers. I was calm and relatively unaffected: because my Spiritual Threads were strong, I was able to focus on what I had rather than what I had lost. I was confident that I would make my money back quickly (and I did).

Once you have hit bottom, the only way is up. This man eventually built a new life for himself, but he had no golden rope up which to climb, and his learning curve was gradual and lengthy.

What his plight brought home to me was that you can have all the material possessions that you have ever dreamed of, without being truly successful.

If you are spiritually unprepared for wealth, it can turn your head in the wrong direction. And if you go so far as to sacrifice your sense of self to worldly possessions or a particular career path, you debase your own spirit and damage your self-esteem. Part 3 of this book, 'The Wealth Threads', showed you how wealth can work for you – rather than the other way round.

When you strengthen your spiritual threads, you can lose 'everything' – and still have everything.

Stepping out

The chapters in this section explore aspects of spirituality for those of you who 'have faith', and those who don't. The methodology may be different but the ambitions, results and benefits are much the same. There are no shortcuts to inner harmony, but there is much that you can do to speed your own progress.

When seeking to develop yourself spiritually, it is all too easy to become insular. It is tempting to bleach out the world around you and turn in upon yourself, as if you are the only person in your life. However, if you do so, you limit your scope for personal development.

Adapt your perspective to the bigger picture. Draw your inspiration from your wider environment: people, places and your own role. It could be as simple as going to visit a neighbour, or becoming involved with a local campaign. You will soon see and feel how your actions can have positive, far-reaching effects for everyone – including you. The action points and worksheet at the end of this chapter will show you what to do.

Not long after I began working at that first health club, I arrived for an early morning workout and found the front door unlocked. Usually it was just the cleaner and me at that time of day, so when I went into the changing room I was surprised to find a pair of jeans and an expensive shirt hung up above a pair of boots and a large canvas sports bag. It occurred to me that this was unusual attire for our cleaner.

When I stepped into the gym and saw who was there, I had to pinch myself because I thought I was dreaming. It was Reg Park: Britain's most famous bodybuilder at the time. Reg Park was best known for playing mythical strongmen in Hollywood films, and making history in 1951 when he became the first British contender to win the Mr Universe title. In our club, his picture was pinned at the bottom of the staircase. He was a hero to us.

Reg told me that he had moved to South Africa, but was in Leeds to visit his parents. Then he invited me to join him for the rest of the workout session. For a keen amateur bodybuilder, as I was then, this was like heaven-sent. Before he returned to his home in South Africa, he came back for three or four more early morning workouts. His contentment with his professional life and his family life shone through. After our workouts he would spend time with me over a protein drink, discussing weight training and nutrition. As we talked, I realised that he was as extraordinary on the inside as he was on the outside. Despite his fame and his standing, Reg was keen to help me – an anonymous young amateur in Yorkshire – to improve myself. His generosity and advice had a great impact upon my life.

The time that I spent with Reg Park inspired me. I wasn't surprised that when he passed away in 2007, his family was deluged with e-mails and letters from those who had had the pleasure of knowing him. The family decided to found the Reg Park Legacy Foundation, to help disadvantaged individuals gain access to sport and training. Reg lived the bigger picture; his vision was so strong, it lives on after his death.

66 Life is a savings account: before you can withdraw the interest, you'll need to make the deposits. 99

We are all affected by the people with whom we mix, for better or for worse. The people with whom you surround yourself are often a good indicator of your spiritual condition. If you are surrounded by acquaintances or hangers-on rather than firm friends, you should consider seeking out new or additional groups of people with whom to associate. The Relationship Threads section, which examines the value of personal relationships, will assist you with this process.

If you aren't already involved with your community in some way, shape or form, get out there and begin giving yourself. When you focus on helping others, or you strive to perform positively within a personal or professional relationship, you gain a greater clarity of vision with regard to your own life. Every positive act you accomplish creates a new Golden Thread that will, over time, become part of a thick, unbreakable Golden Rope.

I rarely lose my temper. I never lose sleep. I don't worry about things. I am surrounded by wonderful people in whom I believe as much as they believe in me. I am confident that if worst came to worst and I lost my material possessions, I could get them back.

My life wasn't always like this. Back when I drank excessively and took drugs to stay awake, I was prone to a violent temper. I was once taken to hospital after breaking my hand on someone's face. I broke his jaw, and my wrist. I had a blackout and couldn't remember afterwards what I had done.

When I set out to lift myself from rock bottom, I realised that my sense of self was so diminished it was barely there. I wasn't happy with myself or my lot, because I didn't have a lot to be happy with. Taking responsibility for my past and future was the first big step; feeding my mind was another. Physical fitness transformed my attitude to life. I stepped back and took in the wider picture and the longer view. It was a period of soul-searching, but eventually I saw that I had everything to gain. As I worked on the other Golden Threads in my life, my outlook became increasingly positive and my Spiritual Threads became stronger too. It was a chicken and egg situation: I'm not sure which came first. I have found that strengthening one Golden Thread often strengthens another in turn.

SUMMARY

o   Your Spiritual Threads are at the centre of all that you are and all that you do. The stronger they are, the greater your potential for achievement in both the short and long term. Make them strong, and these Golden Threads will always be there for you.

o   Spiritual Threads are built around the sense of self: that inner identity that is physically undetectable, always present and in a state of continual change and development.

o   In life, what you give out is what you get back. If you are a positive and contented person, and you go out of your way to help others, you will find that others go out of their way to help you.

o   If your Spiritual Threads are strong, you are at peace with yourself and in a position to face whatever lies around the corner.

ACTION POINTS

1.   When somebody catches your eye in the street or at work, smile at them and bid them the time of day. Smiling is good for all of us: your brain releases endorphins that make you feel good every time you smile. Smiling is contagious. Don't be one of those people who can light up a room just by leaving it. Smiling is the common language of the world.

2.   Take off your headphones. Don't let your iPod 'earbuds' become permanent cranial features. For some people, walking down the street with music blaring into their ears is a way of life. But when you drown yourself in sound, you cut yourself off from the world. If you take your mp3 player with you wherever you go, try leaving it at

home once in a while. If you drive to a thumping bass line from your car stereo, turn it off every now and then. This may be unthinkable at first, but as you become attuned to your surroundings, you will find that what happens around you is both interesting and stimulating.

3. Get into the habit of paying compliments. Cast off your starchy British reserve and find something to praise about everyone you meet. It could be an item of their clothing; it could be a personal or professional achievement. Make sure your compliments are genuine. Don't hold back – pay the compliments to their faces.

4. Honour yourself with dignity. Give yourself worth and esteem, and polish your manners. When you treat someone with courtesy and respect, you show that you value them. They will value you in return. So make eye contact with the shop assistants who serve you, and thank them. If you see someone struggling with a heavy bag, stop and offer to help them. They will feel better for it – and so will you.

WORKSHEET

Think back over your life. When can you remember feeling at your very best? Was it when you were a child, or have you felt your best in more recent years? Pin it down to one event or one moment when you were feeling on top of the world. Describe that moment opposite.

Now look back over what you have written. Wouldn't it be wonderful to have that feeling every day? Capture this special moment from your past and allow yourself to revel in it. Let this good feeling invade every cell in your body. How do you think you could allow yourself a few minutes of such happiness every day? What actions can you take to make this a touchstone in your life? Revisit this feeling whenever you are low.

When was it?

What happened?

Where was it?

How did you feel?

Why did you feel like this?

CHAPTER 19

arry's journey

Y ou don't have to subscribe to a religious faith in order to strengthen your Spiritual Threads. The chapter after this one explores the secular path in greater detail.

Barry is lucky enough to have experienced both perspectives. From the 1960s onwards he built a strong Golden Rope and led an extremely happy and profitable life, only venturing into places of worship for weddings, funerals and christenings.

Then in 1990 he had a life-changing experience, which was so profound that every area of his life was affected overnight.

I wanted to tell you about my experience of faith because, while it might not reflect your feelings, it does show how a strong Spiritual Thread can help you on your journey, no matter what you believe.

My faith has opened me up to my core. It has lent freshness to my life and a sense of newness to everything. As a person of faith, I see myself as a very small speck on the edge of a very big picture – and it's a wonderful view. It excites me and stimulates me. Life is not just about me any more: I take a greater interest in the people who surround me. I love meeting new people, doing new things and taking on challenges. I am contented to my very heart. I do my best to enjoy every minute, every second and every moment of every day.

Faith motivates me. It helps me to move forward, in a positive direction. It gives me an additional sense of purpose, and fortifies the courage with which I follow my convictions.

I found my faith at a time when my business was suffering badly. One night, at the end of a long hard day, I went to bed completely worn out. I then did something unusual for me: I picked up the Bible. It opened at Matthew 7, chapter 7. The page was headed, 'Ask, Seek and Knock'. I began to read.

Ask, and it will be given to you. Seek, and you shall find. Knock, and the door will be open to you.

When I came to the bottom of the page, I put the Bible down and decided to take God at his word. I closed my eyes and walked up to an imagined door. I knocked, and began to pray. So earnest were my feelings, I was aware that it was the first genuine prayer I had ever made. This was a time of need in my life. Within seconds a light flooded through this imagined door and entered my body. A sea of love flowed over me. It was like a gentle tide of healing balm. It enveloped me. My soul yearned for more. This experience was so intense and so sacred; it is beyond my human ability to express it fully. My soul had found its home. Many things happened during and after this spiritual experience, which meant that my life would never be the same again.

As a Christian, I read the Bible regularly and am often inspired by what I find there. When I have questions, I often find answers in its pages. Because I believe that what connects all of us to one another is love, one of the passages that has inspired me most is 1 Corinthians, chapter 13, verses 1–13:

> If I speak in the tongues of men and of angels, but have not love, I am only a resounding gong or a clanging cymbal. If I have the gift of prophecy and can fathom all mysteries and all knowledge, and if I have a faith that can move mountains, but have not love, I am nothing. If I give all I possess to the poor and surrender my body to the flames, but have not love, I gain nothing.
>
> Love is patient, love is kind. It does not envy, it does not boast, it is not proud. It is not rude, it is not self-seeking, it is not easily angered, it keeps no record of wrongs. Love does not delight in evil but rejoices with the

truth. It always protects, always trusts, always hopes, always perseveres.

Love never fails. But where there are prophecies, they will cease; where there are tongues, they will be stilled; where there is knowledge, it will pass away. For we know in part and we prophesy in part, but when perfection comes, the imperfect disappears. When I was a child, I talked like a child, I thought like a child, I reasoned like a child. When I became a man, I put childish ways behind me. Now we see but a poor reflection as in a mirror; then we shall see face to face. Now I know in part; then I shall know fully, even as I am fully known.

And now these three remain: faith, hope and love. But the greatest of these is love.

As you get older it is much easier to stay at home and stick to what and who you know, but my faith has also helped to push me out into the world, into new places and towards new people. It has enabled me to see myself and stretch myself in new ways, strengthening my Spiritual Threads all the while.

For example, I have spent a good deal of time knocking on doors in the evenings, rattling a Christian Aid donation tin. By doing so, I have met all kinds of people on the doorsteps. The questions they have asked about my faith and church have challenged and energised me, and made me think on my feet. I have helped run groups for the Alpha course (details at www.uk.alpha.org) at my local church.

I have also served on my local parish council. In this role, I was occasionally called upon to lead community group sessions, and I also helped to mediate other people's difficulties and challenges. I found that when you are looking after and out for somebody else, you stop brooding upon your own situation. It pales into insignificance, inside a bigger picture.

One of the most valuable benefits of my faith has been a new-found ability to forgive and move on. The first Christmas after my health club business had folded, I was standing at the door of the church with a fellow worshipper. We were a 'welcome team', there to greet visitors and members of the congregation. In the distance I caught sight of a woman making her way down the path, with her husband and two children. I knew this woman. In fact, she had caused me a great deal of aggravation and pain. She was a former employee of mine, whose actions and machinations had been a catalyst in my company's downfall. As you can appreciate, under the circumstances I had no desire to meet and greet her. I hurriedly excused myself, and rushed inside the church. As I stood in front of the altar and said a prayer, the teachings of my faith streamed through my mind. I reconsidered my decision.

I walked back outside, greeted the woman and her husband with a smile and shook their hands. I showed her and her family to their seats. In that moment, my anger towards this woman for the devastation that she had caused was gone. The case was closed, and I was healed. It gave me a tremendous feeling of release, and being able to move on without anger or bitterness meant that I could move on all the more quickly.

In short, my faith has helped me to build an incredibly strong Golden Rope that, through extreme events and situations, has successfully held my life together.

CHAPTER 20

Tune in to your life

The German entrepreneur Frederick Koenig, inventor of the high-speed printing press, once said: 'We tend to forget that happiness doesn't come as a result of getting something we don't have, but rather of recognising and appreciating what we do have'.

Immersed in a consumption-led culture and encouraged to crave products that we do not own, it is easy to lose sight of this message. It doesn't help that everyone is so busy. Too many people allow their lives and emotions to reach fever pitch before they begin listening to what their minds are telling them. They react, rather than respond, to what life deals them. When people die, we say they are 'at rest' – but what a shame it is, that they had to wait that long!

If you are to build robust Spiritual Threads for your Golden Rope, you must be able to relax and 'tune in' to yourself. You can be a person of faith or you can be a committed atheist, but this principle applies to everyone.

66 Great people are the result of great thoughts added to great ethics and great practice. 99

If you can appreciate yourself for who you are, many negative emotions such as stress, greed, anger and jealousy will simply be squeezed out.

Don't be fooled by all the books and 'gurus' with their promises of instant happiness; there are no 'quick fixes'. If there were, this book would never have been written! Spiritual fulfilment is an ongoing process.

The upside is that if you have completed the Action Points set out in the earlier chapters of this book, you have already laid good foundations for a rewarding and enriching journey. What follows are the steps that will enable you to add to your happiness and inner harmony. Your Spiritual Threads will grow gradually – but once they are there, they will serve and support you for life.

The next steps

1. Seek out peace and quiet. Many people are drawn to noise and bustle: they think they 'aren't living' if they aren't on their feet or immersed in crowded social environments. For many of us, however, the opposite is true. Take off on your own and visit quiet, picturesque places. Give your imagination the time, space and freedom it needs to invent your future. You will find that when you separate yourself from the world's distractions, you can hear yourself think. What is more, you will be able to think clearly and deeply. The results: inner calm and improved self-knowledge.

After I decided to leave my old lifestyle behind, I began taking my dog for frequent walks in local woods and parks. I would spend hours in these places, lying on the grass and drifting in and out of sleep, or sitting down and thinking long and hard. When I look back at this turbulent period of my life, I remember it as tranquil. There were few people around and no external noise, but I never felt alone. Stepping away from everyday distractions helped me to step outside of myself: I was able to view my life from above, rather than from within. Because I was calm and relaxed, listening to my own thoughts, I was also able to work through numerous challenges and ideas in my mind. I always returned home refreshed and contented, propelled by a new momentum.

2. If you have children, read to them at bedtime. Encourage them to read back to you. This is an enriching experience, which builds relationships and strengthens the parent–child connection.

Some of my happiest memories are of reading to my children when they were little. My work meant that I was often busy or late home but, no matter how tired I was, whenever possible I made a point of telling them bedtime stories. We all adored Roald Dahl, and our favourite book was *Danny, the Champion of the World*. Reading to them made me feel whole, because there was always so much happiness in the room. It was productive for all of us: it engaged their imaginations, improved their language skills, and trained my focus upon the priorities in my life. In a way the bedtime reading was therapeutic for me: I couldn't help but unwind, and the activity was so rewarding that, while I was reading, I found it impossible to think about anything remotely stressful. The children would fall asleep and I would tip-toe out of the bedroom, filled with love for my family and my life.

3. Wander among history. Visit museums, English Heritage properties, National Trust sites and other places of heritage and interest. Take your time exploring them. Allow your present to be informed by the past: these grand, sumptuous monuments make history palpable. They remove us from our everyday realities and stimulate our imaginations. Take a pad and pen: you may be inspired!

4. Give your time, rather than your money, to charities. The late Hollywood actor Paul Newman led an enriched life, amassing a slew of starring roles and a loving family, but his charitable endeavours ranked among his proudest achievements. He once said, 'I don't look at it as philanthropy; I see it as an investment in the community'. To date, his 'Newman's Own' food range has raised more than $250 million for charities worldwide, including his own 'Hole in the Wall Camps' for children with life-threatening illnesses.

If Paul Newman could find the time to do it, can't you? It's easy enough to toss a quid to the person begging for money on the street, but there are more effective ways to contribute to your community. In today's busy world, your most valuable commodity is your time. Volunteer to help others. You could join the Samaritans (see below), visit the elderly or the housebound, organise sponsored events for a good cause, or go and give a talk at your local school. By 'paying it forward' and improving the lives of those around you, you will feel appreciated and valued. Your community will benefit, and your self-esteem will soar.

5. Get into gardening. It is underrated as a self-improving activity, but a 2005 study found that gardening aids relaxation, improves self-confidence and produces a sense of achievement. Get out into the fresh air, tidy the land and grow foods and flowers from seed. If you don't have a garden of your own, apply for an allotment or grow herbs and flowers in window boxes. If none of these options are viable, join a group like the Guerrilla Gardeners (www. guerrillagardening.org): a collection of volunteer groups scattered around the UK, who go out at night and tend to neglected public spaces such as grass verges and roundabouts. A 'shadowy army of plant lovers', the Guerrilla Gardeners are on a mission to make unattractive, grey neighbourhoods more beautiful places in which to live and work.

6. Mix with your neighbours. If you don't spend time with your neighbours, they are missing out – and so are you. Many elderly people live alone and may not be able to get out very much, but still have plenty to say and would be greatly appreciative of your company. Strengthen your community ties and gain a great deal of personal satisfaction. You could learn a lot, too: older generations have many stories and much hard-won knowledge to impart.

7. **Slow down!** So many of us seem to live at a breakneck pace, dashing from one commitment to another with little time to sit back and enjoy our lives. In addition to seeking out peace and quiet on long walks, make sure that every day brings an opportunity to relax – even if just for 15 minutes – and 'take things easy'. Stick to the speed limit on the motorway, and feel your body relax. If you spend a lot of your time ferrying your kids from activity to activity, try sitting down with them and playing board games, or making one another laugh.

8. **Learn counselling skills and put them to good use in everyday life**. There are many counselling courses on offer and voluntary organisations where you can help. For example in the UK you can obtain details of evening and part-time courses from the British Association of Counselling and Psychotherapy (www.bacp. co.uk). Alternatively, have you considered joining the Samaritans? The charity (www.samaritans.org), which offers a 24-hour telephone counselling service for people in distress, is manned by volunteers who have all completed a training programme.

9. **Tune in**. If you are ever stressed, try this exercise. Tune in to your heart, by closing your eyes and imagining your favourite people standing and smiling in front of you, one after another. In your mind, give each of them a big long hug. Feel your stress drift away.

Facing down challenges

No matter who you are or in which direction you are headed right now, you should be able to incorporate some of these changes into your everyday life. This said, these small but significant actions are more easily said than done. Many of us are busy people and we are used to demanding instant results. When steady improvements are more gradual, it becomes more difficult to stay motivated.

Here are some tips to overcoming common challenges:

1. **Make the most of free days out**. If money is an issue for you right now, read through the Wealth Threads section, which focuses upon getting and keeping wealth. But also note that many of the actions outlined above are free. For example, the National Trust and English Heritage both hold special days every September, when their properties are thrown open to the public without entry fees. In addition, many museums offer free entry all year round.

2. **Turn off your mobile phone**. If you are on a long, thoughtful walk or enjoying some personal time and space, a buzzing, beeping mobile phone is the worst distraction imaginable. Are you likely to miss anything important if you turn it off for an hour or two? The answer is probably 'no'.

3. **Override objectors**. Certain people, when they discover the changes that you are making to your life, will criticise or ridicule you. It's a sad fact of life that these people are discomfited when those around them strive for bigger and better things. If you can keep your eye and your mind on the prize, you'll find it easier to rise above the naysayers.

4. **Turn off the television**. This returns to advice given in the Learning Threads section. Television schedules are cluttered with mind candy, to which we attach undue importance. Should a football game or a home improvement show really take precedence over, say, reading to your child at bedtime? Ensure that your priorities are clearly defined.

5. **Find time**. If you are too busy to slow your pace of life and you don't know how you could find time to build your Spiritual Threads, read the chapter on the Productivity Threads, which focuses upon

productivity. With the right tools, you can transform your work–life balance.

SUMMARY

○ If you are to add robust Spiritual Threads, you must be able to relax and 'tune in' to yourself.

○ If you learn to know and appreciate yourself and what you have, negative emotions such as stress, greed, anger and jealousy will be squeezed out of your life.

○ There are many actions that can be incorporated into your daily life, which will enable you to begin strengthening your Spiritual Threads.

ACTION POINTS

1. After you have read through the above list carefully, browse your local newspaper's listings section and visit your local tourist information office. Make a list of all the galleries, museums, activity centres and other sites of interest in your area. Make dates with these places in your diary.

2. Explore your local area on foot or by bicycle. Many of us are accustomed to settled routines, rituals and orbits, and we tend to spend our time retracing our own footsteps. Even if you live in the same place in which you grew up, you may be surprised to discover new attractions, beauty spots and hidden gems on your doorstep.

3. Introduce yourself to your neighbours. Are there any neighbours to whom you have never spoken? Or recent arrivals in your street? A sound community spirit will serve you well; if you have not already done so, knock on these people's doors and make yourself known.

WORKSHEET

What do you most value about yourself? Complete the list below, as per the example, providing as much detail as you can.

Example

I value my: Imagination

Because: It allows me to see what my life can and will become

I value my _____

Because _____

I value my _____

Because _____

I value my _____

Because _____

I value my _____

Because _____

I value my _____

Because _____

I value my _____

Because _____

I value my _____

Because _____

I value my _____

Because _____

I value my _____

Because _____

I value my _____

Because _____

Conclusion

This way forward ...

We all seek happiness in our lives, but we don't always look in the right places. True happiness does not come with a large bank balance or material 'stuff'. It is the product of a purposeful life, lived with passion and aligned to your highest values, regardless of your financial rewards.

Strength to Strength is not based on any abstract theories; it was created from our lives, driven with passion and purpose. Our mission from the outset was to do so much more than just write a book. We wanted to provide powerful, practical tools for you to find your purpose and values. We believe that in doing this you will find the route to the thing that makes your heart sing and create exciting goals that really inspire you on your journey.

If you are on your way, nothing would give us greater pleasure than to hear your story (you can email us at: info@ yourgoldenthreads.com).

If, on the other hand, you are still searching for that elusive spark to light up your life, you may need to do some more work on putting these ideas into practice. After all, as a wise man once said: 'knowing without doing is not knowing at all'. This might mean giving more time and space to your Workshop assignments and persevering with their creative application to your life. It will be worth it when you find that they open up a whole new world of possibilities.

So, as you go out into the world, with innovation as your backbone, along bright new avenues lit by your gleaming Golden Threads, we wish you all the success that this world has to offer you. Take with you humour, patience and a spirit of good will to all, and who knows how far you will travel and how high you will climb.

May God bless your journey as you allow your passions to shape your future.

Epilogue

Your Golden Threads

Your Golden Threads are precious strands,

Linking your heart with your head and your hands,

Creating new visions with heart and mind

As artists have done since the dawning of time.

Begin to fulfil your heart's desire.

Prepare to set the world on fire.

New milestones will be passed; new bests

Will change your life with far-reaching effects.

Then you will build a Golden Rope,

Giving your life strength, meaning and hope.

With this rope you will be free

To choose your golden destiny.

Now with your Golden Rope in place,

Bow your head and ask for God's grace.

Barry Purcell

Index

If life is what you make it, then making it better starts here.

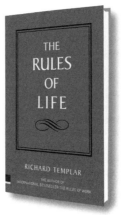

9780273706250

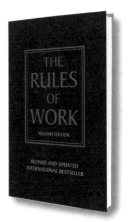

9780273730262

9780273727514

9780273716983

978027372490

Prentice Hall Life books help you to make a change for the better. Together with our authors we share a commitment to bring you the brightest ideas to manage your life, work and wealth.

In these books we hope you'll find the ideas you need for the life you w? Go on, help yourself.

It's what you make it.